Fried Sage

Italian Recipes

&

Cooking Guide for Two

©2019 Cindy Harding Nannarelli

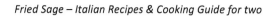

To Andrea & Matteo

Acknowledgements

I thank my husband for being a *buongustaio*

&

Andrea and Matteo

I doubt I would have shared these recipes had my boys not been *buongustaii* too

A Note from the Author

Italy is a country where people have long mastered the art of living life to its fullest. The pleasure of **sharing** a meal with family and friends is first and foremost in most every Italian's life. Italians love food, beauty, and spending time together. This zest for life has been carried on for centuries. It is seen in art as well as books. Just take Botticelli's Venus... the goddess of love rising from the waters on an oyster shell. Oysters were the gourmet delights of the Greeks and Romans. Many festive paintings of banquets dating back centuries have this tantalizing sea faring creature depicted on platters and trays. I believe Italians view food and dining like they view Venus... a goddess on her oyster shell. Italians have tied beauty, food and dining together into one big bow. And this knot cannot be unlaced.

When our youngest son decided to go to college in California and our oldest to relocate to Milan for his first job, I was concerned. Our boys grew up in a home where the importance of good food shared at the table with family and friends was a norm. And it was mom who cooked every night. How would they adapt to cooking for themselves? Would they end up eating fast food and losing their *buongustaio* tastebuds? *Buongustaio* is someone who knows and appreciates good home cooked food. My biggest concern was our youngest son Matteo. Would he take the time to make a savory, pesto pasta, or fry up some sage and zucchini blossoms? Or would he go out for a burger once he moved to California?

To make sure Matteo would stay on the right track, I decided to compile a few simple recipes for both him and his brother, Andrea. Hopefully they would be tempted to strap on aprons and make a Tuscan meal for themselves, and maybe even for others. My goal was to show how cooking at home is fast and easy. All they had to do was take the time to stop at the grocery store on the way home and pick up the ingredients before stepping into their kitchens to prepare a meal reminiscent of home... a meal that carried the flavors of Tuscany.

So there I was, secretly stuffing recipe cards between my son's shirts and socks as he packed. Hoping, when they resurfaced in California, he would put them to good use. Although Matteo seldom donned an apron at home, I felt positive that living abroad would change that. Being a *buongustaio*, I was sure he would get tired of fast food very fast. And I was right, for just weeks after moving he emailed home for more easy recipes. His criteria: fast and simple recipes for two. Recipes like *tiramisu,* a dessert he made the weekend before. He proudly commented, "It was a hit!" The girls next door, albeit four blondes from Sweden and not California, asked him to make the dessert for a party they were planning the following weekend. One of the girls asked if he might even make her an authentic Florentine meal one evening. It was a date. He needed a menu.

Seeing how Matteo was successfully reeling in girls with his culinary knowhow, his long-time friend and roommate, Jake, decided to step up to the plate as well. An avid football player, Jake was accustomed to strapping on kneepads and helmets, I venture he never thought he'd be donning an apron once he got to college. But like any athlete who finds himself in a win-win situation, he was smart to take the ball and run with it.

In the months that followed, both Matteo and his brother Andrea were emailing home for recipes and cooking advice. Their culinary questions were... "What can I serve with lemon chicken?" "What goes better with pork - Beans or potatoes?" I especially enjoyed the email in which our youngest son, the one who barely touched vegetables and absolutely HATED eggplant, asked me for my ricotta-stuffed eggplant recipe. Matteo must be dating a vegetarian, I told my husband.

It comforted me to know both our boys had embraced cooking. They were quick to realize how much money they were saving by eating at home as opposed to eating out. Besides, with just a bit of practice they were whipping up two and three course meals in less than an hour. Not that they were making three course meals every night, but at least they had the tools in the event they wanted to. So, after a series of culinary calls back and forth between Florence and Santa Barbara, and Florence and Milan, I decided to sit down and put together a book of three course meals, complete with shopping lists and step-by-step preparation outlines.

By incorporating three recipes into one easy plan. All the boys had to do was grab what was on the shopping list for the meal they wanted to prepare, run to the grocery store and come back and strap on an apron. And, once they understood the steps in preparing any given dish, they could pluck recipes from individual menus to mix and match, thus creating their own menu. All I had to do was choose dishes with ingredients I knew the boys liked and that were easily available. To further encourage the guys to don an apron, I decided to toss a bit of spice into the mix by including ingredients with some zesty folklore, like tidbits on natural aphrodisiacs that could serve as enticing table conversation.

I opted to entitle the collection *Fried Sage* being these tasty finger food nibbles, together with fried zucchini blossoms, are favorites in our home.

About the Menus & Recipes

Simplicity, coupled with a desire to entice, were key when deciding which recipes to include in the menus. Ingredient accessibility, together with the cost factors was also important. Having sons with diverse palates, one a meat-and-potato kind of guy, the other a fruit and veggie lover, made it easy for me to diversify. Thus offering a range of tasty dishes for all palates.

The fact that Matteo was in college, gave me the idea of organizing the chapters into: Freshman, sophomore, junior and senior segments. Although the menus and recipes in the freshman and sophomore segments tend to ease one into the second group, all the recipes are simple and easy to make. I chose to begin each chapter with a theme. Each theme is based on facts and/or folklore. The freshman and sophomore menus begin with an antipasto and are followed by a first course and entrée. The junior and senior year menus start with first courses and continue onto entrées paired with side dishes. If one wishes to add an antipasto to any of these menus, just pluck one from either of the first two years. In fact, once the procedure for making a particular dish has been mastered, I encourage mixing and matching (i.e. taking recipes from one menu and tossing them into another), especially when one has the ingredients already on hand. It's easy to built menus around ingredients sitting in the pantry or in the fridge. You'd be surprised what you can do with a can of tomatoes, a can of beans and a can of tuna when fresh herbs are growing in pots on your windowsill. I know, you're probably thinking, "wait that is too much trouble! Herbs growing in my windowsill?" But remember, Italian/Mediterranean food is all about freshness even when using staples from the cupboard. Consider how convenient it is to pluck a few leaves of basil from a potted plant growing on your windowsill and tossing it into a bubbling tomato sauce. Not only is the aromatic herb filling your kitchen with the aroma of Tuscan life, it is giving you a superb sauce. For that burst of freshness allows your creation to sing! It is surely worth that minute or two it takes to water those plants before going to bed for what they give back. Besides, growing your own herbs will save you money. They are tastier and cheaper than buying fresh herbs or dried herbs from your local grocery store.

Following each chapter introduction are the menus, each with a complete and comprehensive shopping list of all the ingredients needed to make the complete. I designed the menus for two, but sometimes you might have to buy more than what is needed for an intimate *tête-à-tête* dinner due to packaging. No worries, keep the extra ingredients on hand. You can either store them in the fridge or freeze them. You are sure to put them to good use. Or simply double the ingredients in the recipes and invite more people to dinner.

Both the shopping lists and outlines (advance and final preparation) are built around the three dishes in each menu). So, if you'd like to make just one of the dishes, read the plan first so you can identify the ingredients needed for that dish. By following the plans step by step, you can have a savory three-course meal on the table in less than an hour in most cases.

At the end of the sixteen menu plans (or forty-eight recipes), I have included three desserts; one for coffee lovers, one for fruit connoisseurs and one for those who adore the world's most famed aphrodisiac - rich dark chocolate. I venture to say knowing how to prepare these decadent three is plenty to entice.

Remember, cooking can be fast and easy. It is rewarding in more ways than one. Take it from fun-loving Italians who have known for centuries that one of life's simplest pleasures is cooking and dining with family and/or friends. It is time to venture into the world of *buongustaii*. Strap on that apron and make your taste buds dance.

Before Getting Down to the Nitty-Gritty

Utensils to have on hand

Before creating any culinary masterpiece (and a savory gastronomic delight is just that) make sure you have all the necessary equipment within reach. Below is a list of the things that will make life in the kitchen easier. So, before setting out to conquer the world of cooking make sure to set the stage. If you don't already have these items in the kitchen pick them up.

1) A small electric food processor or grinder.

2) A mini-primer (hand blender). This handy gadget enables you to whip up creamy pâtés and mayonnaise in seconds.

3) One or two sharp chef knives & a few smaller knives

4) A cutting board

5) A pair of scissors

6) 2 frying pans (10-inch, and one smaller)

7) 2 or 3 saucepans (1 to 3 quarts) with lids

8) One large pasta pot (4 to 6 quarts) with lid

9)   One strainer or colander (for pasta)

10) One rectangular baking dish & at least four cupcake forms

11) A large mixing bowl

12) A set of measuring cups

13)

Staples to have around

Pasta: short, long, thin. Rich in carbohydrates, low in fat (when dressed properly) and quick to prepare, pasta is an all-around great choice for a first course. Some varieties of whole grain pasta pro-vide up to 25% of one's daily fiber requirement in just one cup. The important thing to remember when making pasta, especially if one is watching weight, is to keep the sauce simple. The recipes in this compilation are all dressed with easy-to-make, savory sauces.

Rich in healthy aphrodisiacs, each dish is a great source of energy **without** being fattening. When you keep a pasta simple, like the one in the first recipe – *Pasta Carrettiera,* you would have to indulge in at least four servings to equal the same amount of calories you'd be consuming if you were sitting down to a double burger and fries instead of pasta. So why not fill up on this Mediterranean favorite? Pasta is not only the choice first course of Italians. it's the food of athletes as well.

Olive Oil: King of the Mediterranean Pantry. Although a good olive oil can be costly, there are tasty choices priced for a student's budget. The important thing to look for when choosing olive oil is its color. When an olive oil boasts the color of golden hay, more than likely it has been mixed with other oils, possibly canola or sunflower seed. Many of these oils are labeled as Pure Olive Oil. A strange name for an oil mix, wouldn't you say? It's the extra virgin first cold press label you should be looking for. When cold-pressed the oil, like the olives, is green. So when selecting oil, make sure it has this green hue. There are excellent choices coming out of Italy, mainly Tuscany, as well as Spain, Greece and California. And remember, even if you find it hard to justify paying the same amount of money for a bottle of oil as you might pay for a pizza, just remember how many savory dishes you'll be putting on the table, night after night, with that one bottle! *Note:* Store oil in a dark, cool spot away from sun and heat. If stored correctly, olive oil can last up to a year or more.

Canned Items: I suggest having the following in your cupboard, as they can be lifesavers when that special someone just happens to knock on the door right around dinner.

Canned tomatoes (simple with no added vegetables)- Plain stewed

Canned tomato sauce (plain with no added herbs or vegetables)

Canned tuna (water or oil-packed)

Canned or bottled white beans – cannellini or haricot

Vegetable bouillon (cube, granular or liquid)

Capers

Red wine vinegar

Balsamic vinegar

Flour 00

Vegetable oil (sunflower seed for frying)

Apart from having the above staples in your cupboard, it's always good to have a few fresh items in the **fridge** as well. I suggest you always have eggs, butter, salad greens and tomatoes on hand. For together with a few selected cupboard staples, these ingredients allow you to put together a quick, tasty dish together when time is precious or when some-one pops in unexpected.

Herbs

Being I live in Tuscany, many of the recipes in this collection reflect this area's cuisine. And being that the ethos of Tuscan gastronomy is exquisitely fresh and seasonal, the use of fresh herbs is a must. I am well aware that in countries like my native America, growing herbs for culinary use, as Europeans do, isn't that widespread, especially among college students or young working adults. But considering how expensive herbs can be, I would re-think this option. For without the use of fresh herbs in your dishes, they just won't sing. So...allow me to reiterate. Why not go to your local nursery and buy a handful of potted herbs? Having a small herb garden on your balcony or windowsill will not only give your dishes the freshness they deserve, it will add a Mediterranean flair to your *casa*. Just remember to water these aromatic plants! Below is a list of the fresh herbs I can't live without:

Basil (used for sauces and vegetables); **Bay leaves** (good in sauces and stews); **Oregano** (great for tomato sauces and fish); Parsley (it goes here, there and everywhere); **Rosemary** (used for vegetables, poultry and fish); Sage (used for chicken and potatoes); **Thyme** (used for veggies, soups, sauces); **Parsley** (Italian parsley is great with fish dishes)

Note: Garlic, as well as onions should always be on hand.

Aphrodisiacs – healthy yet enticing ingredients

Folklore or fact, most scientific studies relating to aphrodisiacs have turned up fruitless when looking for evidence that any given food carries a miracle potion in its chemistry. Having said this, a group of American and Italian scientists DID inadvertently discover the exist-ence of a rare amino acid found in Mediterranean mussels that showed how the sexual hormone levels in rats were raised by this acid. To my knowledge, however, since these 2005 findings no fur-ther studies have been conducted to add further insight into their findings. Nonetheless, despite the lack of scientific proof, one varie-ty of crustaceans has been leading the list of culinary aphrodisiacs for centuries. But it isn't simply shellfish. A number of spices and vegetables are considered just as enticing. Below is a list of foods whose nutritional benefits are as tantalizing as their fame.

Almonds

Chock a block full of vitamin E, magnesium and fiber this tiny fruit (yes, almonds are fruit) have long been associated with fertility. It has been said that the simple aroma of almond has the power to awaken female passion. It is no wonder almond oil is a favorite; even when it comes to massages.

Asparagus

A great source of vitamins B6, A and C, thiamin and folic acid, aspar-agus is claimed to boost the production of histamine. I read that in

19th century France bridegrooms were served a three-course meal of asparagus the evening before their nuptials. Could these sexy spears indeed have the power to stir up lust?

Avocados

Rich in vitamin B6, potassium and folic acid avocados have been associated with radiant health for centuries. But did you know that this odd-shaped fruit, known as *ahuacuatl* to the ancient Aztecs, was associated with sexuality as well? Hanging in pairs from the tree, the Aztecs were quick to note the fruit's resemblance to... Let's leave it to one's imagination.

Bananas

Due to their shape, bananas are obviously connected to sexuality. Containing minerals and the bromelain enzyme, this fruit (as well as pineapple) is famed as a natural male libido enhancer. Bananas were also said to have been the fruit of choice for women looking for pleasure tools in days gone by. A healthy, pleasurable fruit one might say.

Basil

During Roman times this fragrant herb was considered a symbol of love. This is no wonder considering its sweet aroma and pleasing taste. In addition to this fame, basil also provides our bodies with a good supply of Vitamin C, betacarotene, magnesium and potassium. All of which are considered libido-lifting nutrients.

Carrots

Like bananas, this phallus shaped vegetable has been associated with seduction for centuries. And like basil, carrots are jam-packed with high levels of vitamins and betacarotene. Carrots were not only popular aphrodisiacs in Ancient Greece. They were considered highly in the Arab world as well. In fact the Arabs were known to boil carrots in milk before serving the beverage to those in need. This drink has the power to improve mucous membranes. Making it a natural lubricant. Who says carrots are only good for your eyes?

Chili peppers

The capsaicin in chili peppers gets our hearts beating as pleasurable endorphins are released into our system. To get blood racing, mix one of these little devils with the next ingredient on the list.

Chocolate

Whether science eventually ends up proving the aphrodisiac powers of any given food, I doubt chocolate will lose its position as "King of the Natural Aphrodisiacs," alongside oysters. With its makeup of PEA (phenylethylamine), a chemical that discharges dopamine into the pleasure centers of the brain, coupled with tryptophan (a key component of serotonin) another brain chemical related to sexual arousal, I doubt chocolate's fame will be tarnished anytime soon.

Coffee

Caffeine has the power to stimulate both body and mind, but too much turns coffee into a depressant. This can be a real downer when planning a romantic evening dinner for two. So don't go overboard with coffee. Make a tiramisu instead.

Figs

One of the world's oldest recorded fruits, figs have been tied to female sex organs ever since… Eve. Is it or is it not a fig leaf seen covering certain parts? Some writings go so far as to insinuate an open fig actually mimics these organs. But Eve wasn't the only woman in history reaching out to a fig for help. Cleopatra had a fondness for figs as well. Rumor had it her servants brought figs and water to her chambers every morning.

Garlic

In Buddhist traditions, garlic is believed to stimulate desires by warming the body. Known as the 'stinking rose,' this pearly bulb does increase blood flow. But despite this healthier aspect of garlic, it's probably not at the top of shopping lists when planning a romantic meal for two. Right? But shying away from this pungent condiment for fear of 'garlic breath' is a big mistake, especially when it can be paired with parsley, an herb with the power of temporarily masking garlic's overpowering taste. So if you're planning to embrace the Italian way, stock up on garlic and make sure fresh parsley is always in the fridge or growing on your windowsill. Do as Italians do, sprinkle the leafy herb here, there and everywhere; and don't forget the breath mints!

Honey

Made from the nectar of flowers, this natural sugar is as sensuous as it is delectable. Try licking it off one's fingers! Gathered by honeybees, this sweet, sticky substance is a great source of the trace mineral boron. A mineral said to help metabolize the female sex hormone estrogen. But honey isn't limited to enhancing only one hormone. It is equally known to boost testosterone levels. Try drizzling a bit of this gooey delight atop a sliver of cheese and wait to see how your taste buds buzz.

Oysters

It wasn't only the goddess of love who contributed to making these mollusks legendary. Back in the second century AD, the Roman satirical poet Juvenal helped this cause. In one of his writings, he wrote, *"for what does a drunken woman regard; she knows not the difference between her top or bottom; she who eats raw oysters at midnight."* By the mere mentioning of drunken women and raw oysters in the same stanza, Juvenal obviously managed to portray oysters as potent aphrodisiacs. But whether this fame oysters have acclaimed has merit or not, if one's budget allows, serve an oyster now and then. You needn't serve them nude on the half shell. They are just as tantalizing *au-gratin*. Or combine fresh oysters and their juice with cooked spinach, a few spices and a creamy white sauce. Stuff the half shells and pop them in the oven, or under the broiler. You will be sure to make that all important *'bella figura,'* (good impression) as Italians say.

Pine Nuts

These tiny seeds, found nudged inside of pinecones, have been linked to the stimulation of male libido for centuries. They are high in zinc, a mineral necessary for maintaining male potency. Sprinkle roasted pine nuts atop salads. Grind them with basil when making a pesto. Or simply pop a few in your mouth while preparing dinner. The subtle taste of these pearly gems will add flair to an array of dishes.

Shrimp

Rich in omega-3 fatty acids and elevated levels of iodine, once ingested, these tiny sea creatures break down into phenylalanine, a powerful amino acid that sends good endorphins to the brain. So, stock up on shrimp when it goes on sale at your local fish market. You can easily freeze the little creatures when bought fresh. Grilled them, sauté them, or simply boiled and tossed into a salad.

Strawberries

It's no wonder strawberries, with their perfect heart-shaped bodies, were associated with Venus during the time of the Roman Empire. High in vitamin C, pair them with a flute of sparkling wine for the perfect icebreaker. Strawberries are great to end a meal. Try feeding a few strawberries dipped in warm dark chocolate or smothered in fresh whipped cream to that special someone and see where it gets you.

Thyme

Besides its fame of possessing extraordinary aphrodisiacal powers, the tiny leaves of this small green shrub are said to make a powerful tonic for nerves. Truth or myth... among the 100 versions of this herb (part of the mint family), it has the power to transform any dish it marries with into a culinary delight.

Truffles (Oil or Salt)

I wholeheartedly doubt my readers, especially students, will have either the funds or time to get their hands on even the tiniest of these black or white tubers known as truffles. However, buying truffle oil or salt is a whole different story. Both are available in specialty gourmet stores. And since only the slightest hint of this rarity is bound to arouse, the musky aroma of this condiment might be something to have on hand. Both truffle salt and oil will last a long time. Try seasoning a chicken breast with truffle salt while grilling, or adding a few drops of truffle oil to a batch of creamy mashed potatoes. Just letting your date know truffles are savory tubers and not chocolate might win you some brownie points!

Wine

Through the alchemy of grapes, wine is a beverage possessing the power to arouse our senses. But like coffee, it also has the power to put a huge damper on an evening when it is abused. The "nectar of gods" should be treated with the respect it deserves. This is something Italians know well. Like most Europeans, wine is paired with food. A *buongustaio* (one who appreciates good food and drink) savors the wine as much as the food it is paired with. Italians do not drink wine to get drunk. It is an important part of their meal. It is to be savored.

And now for the menus...

Freshman Year - We Are What We Eat

Living in a city like Florence, with its numerous university programs, our home has seen its share of international students. Upon finding themselves at our dining table, both girls and boys always seem to ask the same question... "How can Italians eat so much and still be thin?" The answer is: Italians eat well. They eat with purpose and in moderation. Much like Leonardo Da Vinci professed: do not eat if you are not hungry; eat lightly; drink wine in moderation – not on an empty stomach or between meals... By eating well, Italians, like Da Vinci, believe in using fresh and seasonal ingredients in the preparation of all dishes. By purpose, they mean almost always sitting down to share a meal with family and/or friends over stimulating conversation. For food, family and friends are the ingredients that make life worth living. Food is life's simplest pleasure. It should be savored. Although Italians do indulge in multi-course meals, sometimes on a daily basis, it is always in moderation. Couple this with the known fact that Italians, like most Europeans, walk daily, it is no wonder many Italians sport radiant health.

But let's take a look at what Italians are eating. We all know food gives us energy, and the chief sources of energy are in FATS, CARBOHYDRATES and PROTEINS. Protein is the primary source of body-building. The word itself, stemming from the Greek word 'to come first,' tells us how important protein is for building and maintaining our bodies. Some protein is better than others, especially when it comes to nutrition and calorie counting. But the best quality protein is found in cheese, eggs, fish, meat and milk, all of which Italians have on their tables regularly.

Now let's take a quick look at FATS. They contain more calories per unit of weight than carbohydrates. Olive oil, which contains roughly 119 calories per tablespoon, is the good fat Italians take in on a daily basis. With its monounsaturated fatty acids, olive oil is a healthy dietary fat choice. Butter and heavy creams are used sparingly, at least in Italian-Tuscan cuisine. These fats are considered the 'not so good' fats. One might ask why? Especially when a tablespoon of butter contains a few less calories than the same tablespoon of olive oil (102 versus 119). But butter has 11 grams of fat in that tablespoon, not monounsaturated fatty acids. So with its negligible amount of protein, carbohydrates and its lack of fiber, butter is practically fat! Thus making extra virgin cold press olive oil a much healthier choice. Although Frenchmen may not agree!

So how do Italians make up for their limited intake of fatty fats if they inevitably choose olive oil over butter in cooking? Easy, they take in a fair amount of carbohydrates. Bread and pasta are staples found on dining tables up and down the peninsula on a daily basis. And again, both are made of whole grains, i.e. good fiber choices. Italians buy freshly baked bread daily.

They seldom resort to pre-packaged or processed breads. Traditional Tuscan bread is salt less, which means it stales in 24 hours or so. But this is not a bad thing. Tuscan day old bread is used to make *panzanella* (bread and fresh veggie salads), *ribollita* (bread and vegetable soup), and *pappa al pomodoro* (bread, tomato, garlic and fresh basil mush). All of these renowned dishes could not be made without this stale bread.

And now for a word about the menus that follow: Keeping in mind the eating habits my sons have been accustomed to growing up in Italy, I have put together the following sixteen menus. They are in no way designed to provide the ideal amounts of carbohydrates, protein or fat in any given meal. I am certainly not qualified to offer such information. But having a minimum savvy in regards to nutrition, I tried to pair dishes that not only brought out the best in one another, but were healthy and enticing choices as well. For isn't that what life is all about, bringing out the best in something, or someone? Although you won't find a bubbling hot polenta paired alongside a basket of Tuscan bread (both corn meal and wheat like to take center stage and we all know that two *prima donna's* seldom share the same table...). However, you will find a more refined carbohydrate like white rice possibly paired with a fatty cheese. So, if a mouthwatering delight like *risotto a quattro formaggi* (Four Cheese Risotto) seems tempting, just keep portion control in mind if you are watching your weight. So, if you're ready. Let's start cooking!

Menu One: Artichoke Canapés - Spicy *Carretti-era* Pasta - Grilled Chicken smothered in Fresh Spring Greens & Dressed in a Balsamic Vinaigrette

Shopping - Ingredients to pick up

One jar of plain marinated artichoke hearts in packed in oil

A small container of cream cheese

One loaf of hard crusted French bread

One 14.28 oz (400 g) can of Italian plum or cherry tomatoes (simple with no herbs added)

One 6 oz can of tomato paste

One bulb of fresh garlic - at least 5 cloves

A handful of fresh parsley

Red hot pepper flakes

One package n° 5 spaghetti (a universal Italian brand)

One large chicken breast

One package of Italian mix salad greens

Olive oil

Balsamic vinegar

Salt & pepper

Advance preparation

1. Toss marinated artichokes into electric chopper. If you have fresh thyme on hand toss in a sprig. Puree. Transfer pureed artichokes into a small bowl. Add a tbsp of olive oil. Stir, cover and put aside. Clean chopper.

2. Remove skin from garlic cloves. Toss two cloves, together with parsley (a hand full), into the chopper. Give it a whirl. Put mince into a small bowl, put aside. Clean chopper. Put aside the three remaining whole cloves.

3. Take out a chef's knife and cutting board. Take chicken breast. Rinse, pat dry and place on cutting board. With sharp knife, divide breast into two halves – a vertical cut down the middle. Now slice each half horizontally without making a clean cut through the half breast. This will open the half. Lightly press the open half down with knife's body. Repeat operation with second half of breast. Now you have two fillets. Put them aside. Carefully wash cutting board and knife with soap and water. Put away.

4. Make vinaigrette: In a blender put 3/4 cups of olive oil, 3 tablespoons balsamic vinegar, salt and pepper to taste. Blend for 30 seconds. Now pour vinaigrette into a small bottle or cup. It will keep up to one week. Clean blender.

5. Take out a stovetop grill if you have one, or the broiling pan from the oven. Take out a large pasta pot (4 - 6 quart size). Fill it 3/4 full of water. Turn on heat so water will boil.

6. Set Table. See Sophomore Year Introduction on Setting the Table and Mood. Remember you will be eating in courses so you will need a pasta bowl and dinner plate, and possibly a dessert plate that morphs into an antipasto dish.

Final Preparation & Presentation of

Artichoke Heart Canapés

Slice **French bread** into 6 or 8 rounds (3 or 4 - 1 inch canapé slices). Spread each slice with **cream cheese**. Now take the bowl of puréed artichokes and spread the pâté atop the cheese canapés. Arrange each slice on a serving dish (a plate will do). If you have a lemon in the house, grate some zest (the yellow peel, not the white inner part) atop. It makes for a great garnish as well as adding a hint of lemon. Also sprinkle a few thyme leaves here and there.

Your antipasto is ready to serve. This can be prepared in advance. Great finger food to enjoy with a glass of wine.

Spicy *Carrettiera* Pasta

Pull out large frying pan (which morphs into a sauté pan). Add 1/4 cup of olive oil. Cut the three remaining garlic cloves into halves and toss them into pan. Turn on heat and allow garlic to sauté for a couple of minutes (don't let it burn or get too crispy). Remove cloves when golden, and disregard them. Open can tomatoes, drain liquid into a glass and toss tomatoes into the pan. Add one tablespoon of tomato paste to the tomato water in the glass. Stir. You should have a tomato sauce of medium consistency. If too watery, add a bit more paste. Pour this sauce into pan. Now sprinkle salt atop (at least a heaping teaspoon - Italians love salt!) Allow tomatoes and sauce to simmer on medium heat for 10 minutes. Lower heat and toss in 1/2 tsp of red hot pepper flakes (or one chili pepper broken into pieces) along with half of the minced parsley and garlic you prepared earlier. Stir in and allow sauce to simmer for another 10 minutes before turning off heat. Cover pan.

By this time the pasta water should have reached a rolling boil. Toss in 2 (yes two) tablespoons of salt (preferably rock salt but regular salt will do). Now toss in half the package of pasta. Remember, 100 grams of pasta per person is sufficient. Italians usually calculate 80 grams per serving. Allow pasta to cook to its *al dente* stage. This means if 11 minutes is written on package as cooking time, do not cook longer. Actually strain pasta one minute earlier.

IMPORTANT: when straining pasta ALWAYS keep aside a cup of the starchy pasta water aside (just dip a cup into the pot to collect water before straining pasta). If you think you have too much sauce to dress the pasta, remove some of the sauce. Put aside for another dinner. Figure that 1/2 cup of sauce is sufficient per portion.

Now toss the strained noodles into the sauce. Turn on heat and using two folks, mix noodles into sauce, or if you want to try flipping the pasta inside the sauce to amalgamate both, that is fine too. Just don't flip the pasta out of the pan! Add a bit of the starchy pasta water if pasta looks a bit dry. This will add creaminess to the sauce and allows the sauce and noodles to marry. Sprinkle the remaining parsley and fresh garlic mince atop. Give the pasta one last mix. Serve.

IMPORTANT: pasta is to be served immediately while it is still *al dente* – firm but not hard on the outside and slightly but enjoyably chewy on the inside. Waiting around will only serve to make pasta soft and mushy... NOT an authentic Italian experience.

Hint: Once you sit down to enjoy your finger food canapés this is the time to toss pasta into boiling water. Don't forget the salt! Pasta water should taste like seawater.

Grilled Chicken smothered in Fresh Greens

This is a dish that can be prepared even before your guest arrives, especially if you have a microwave in the kitchen.

Prepare grill or turn on broiler part of oven. Salt and pepper chicken breasts on both sides, sprinkle them with a few drops of balsamic vinegar and a light drizzle of olive oil. Rub the oil and vinegar, salt and pepper on the chicken using your hands. Now place the half breasts on the grill or under broiler. Wash hands with soap and water while allowing breasts to char to a golden color on both sides. Remove chicken from the grill or oven. Turn off heat. Transfer breasts to a platter. Cover for a minute or two, allowing juices to ease from chicken. Now place breasts on cutting board and slice them into strips (each 1/2 breasts should allow for at least five long strips). Place strips back on platter. If you grilled the chicken earlier and it is now room temperature, stick the platter into the micro for a minute. If you grilled the fowl while the pasta noodles were cooking, then the strips should still be warm. Now sprinkle salad greens atop the chicken and dress the greens with the vinaigrette you previous prepared. Crack black pepper atop. Serve alongside a basket of warm bread.

Note: For those choosing to serve wine with the meal, I would go with a fruity or dry white wine. Make sure it is chilled.

Menu Two: Tuna Canapés - Homemade Pesto Pasta - Broiled Fish (Tilapia or other fish fillet) Smothered in Grilled Veggies

Prep Time: 30 minutes; Total grilling time: 15 -18 minutes.

Shopping – Ingredients to pick up

One can of white albacore tuna packed in water or oil

A small bottle of capers

Butter

One loaf of French bread

One 13 oz package of gnocchi or a package of penne or bow pasta

One package of grated Parmesan cheese

One large bunch of fresh basil

One small package of pine nuts (or walnuts)

Olive oil

1 clove garlic

2 fish fillets (4 if they are small)

A small basket of cherry tomatoes

One white or yellow onion (medium size)

2 or 3 long zucchini

Fresh Thyme

Advance Preparation

1. Drain tuna from oil or water and toss into food processor along with 2 tbsp butter and 1 tbsp olive oil. Add a sprig of thyme leaves or parsley, whichever is on hand. Toss in a ta-blespoon of capers. Now whip ingredients into a smooth spread. Put paste into bowl, cover and put aside. Clean processor and put it away.

2. Pull out blender or mini primer. Blender the following: one heap of fresh basil leaves (at least 2 packed cups), 1/3 cup of pine nuts or walnuts; 1/2 cup of grated Parmesan cheese (Reggiano or Romano will also do); 1/2 cup extra virgin olive oil; 1 garlic clove; salt and pepper to taste. Add a bit more oil if consistency is too dense. Pour pesto into bowl or cup. Set aside. This recipe yields one large cup of pesto. Clean blender and put it away.

3. Pull out cutting board and knife. Peel onion. Clean zucchini. Slice 1/2 the onion into thin 1/8 inch-thick circles. The other half you can put away for another dish. Now julienne zucchini (this means slicing them lengthwise into 1/8 inch-slices). Now take 10 cherry tomatoes and slice them in half. Place vegetables on a tray, sprinkle salt, pepper and fresh thyme atop the lot. Drizzle with olive oil, mix with hands so all veggies are coated. Set aside. Clean board and knife.
4. Pull out fish fillets. Wash and pat dry. Season both sides of fillets with salt and pepper. Sprinkle fresh thyme or oregano atop. Drizzle with olive oil. Allow fillets to marinate for 30 min.

Final Preparation & Presentation of

Tuna Canapés

Slice French bread into 4 or 6 rounds (2 or 3 canapés each). Spread each slice with the creamy tuna/caper spread. Top each canapé with a caper. Arrange on a serving dish. If you have a lemon on hand, grate zest (yellow lemon rind) atop. Place a fresh parsley sprig alongside canapés for decoration. These are finger foods so can be eaten with napkins or served on an antipasto plate alongside any of the other canapés in the recipes that follow. In Italy many times three different canapés are served together. This is known as a *tris.*

Pasta with Homemade Pesto

Put large pot of water (at least 4 quarts) on the heat to boil. Pull out pesto and pour 1/2 a cup into a large serving bowl. Add a couple of fresh basil leaves, a tablespoon of pine nuts and one tablespoon of olive oil. Set aside. Once water reaches a rolling boil, toss in 2 tablespoons of salt. Now, if you are using store bought fresh gnocchi, drop them into the water and be ready to fish them out once they have popped to the surface. If, on the other hand, you have opted for penne pasta or a bow shaped pasta, it will take roughly 10 minutes to reach the pasta's *al dente* stage, giving you time to work on the entrée. Once pasta is ready to drain, dip a coffee cup into the starchy pasta water and fill it before straining pasta. Now toss the strained pasta into the bowl of pesto, add 1/2 the starchy water and mix sauce and pasta together. I usually add a bit more of the starchy water to cream up the sauce. Add a bit more pesto if need be as well. The remaining pesto can be saved in the fridge. It lasts for a couple of days at least. Serve immediately.

Broiled Fish Fillets smothered in Grilled Veggies

Pull out broiler pan from oven. If you have aluminum foil or parchment paper on hand, line the pan. Arrange the julienne zucchini, onions and cherry tomatoes atop and place under a pre-heated broiler. Keep an eye on the veggies so they don't get too crispy or burnt. Turn them over midway between broiling. You should pull them out when they seem to be 3/4 of the way done. This should be about 8-10 minutes.

Note: this is something you can even do before the guest arrives, as you will be sticking the veggie back in the oven with the fish anyway.

Now top the veggies with the marinated fish fillets. Pop the lot back under the broiler and allow the fish to broil on both sides until it turns flaky white and its juices begin to settle into the veggies. This should take a few minutes on both sides. Remove the fish and veggies from under the broiler. Carefully remove fillets to a platter or individual dishes using a wide spatula. If the veggies still look like they could use a bit more color then pop them under the broiler for a couple more minutes. Cover the fish in the meantime. Once the veggies have a slightly golden color to them, smother the fish with these savory grilled veggies while pouring any juices that are left in pan atop the fish and veggies. Serve alongside a spring salad dressed in olive oil & wine or apple vinegar.

Amatriciana (Bacon & Onion) Spaghetti- Grilled Pork Medallions on Peppery Arugula

Total Prep Time: less than 30 minutes; Cooking time: 15 – 20 minutes

Shopping – Ingredients to pick up

One can of black olives (pitted)

One small package of cream cheese

One sprig of fresh Thyme or Oregano

A couple bulbs of garlic

Olive oil

4 strips of lean (non-smoked) bacon

One medium yellow onion

One package of n° 5 spaghetti (only half a pack is needed for 2)

Red hot pepper flakes

One 14.28 oz (400 g) can of plain Italian plum or cherry tomatoes, meaning no herbs added to tomatoes. Brands like Cento, Carmelita, Marconi, Nina San Marzano or Contadina are good choices.

One lean pork loin roast (when selecting piece remember you will be cutting the roast into 1 inch rounds so imagine how many rounds you would like to serve (2 to 3 should suffice per person).

Fresh Rosemary

One lemon

Arugula or Spring Mix Salad Greens

Advance Preparation

1. Pull out chopper. Open canned olives. Drop them into chopper along with one clove of garlic and one sprig of thyme. Give them a whirl until they are finely minced. Scoop mince into a bowl. Add 1/4 cup of olive oil. Mix until you have a uniform, creamy yet dense, paste. Add a drop of oil, if needed, to reach consistency. Taste for salt. Put aside. Clean chopper.

2. Pull out chopping block and knife. Cut bacon slices into one inch wide pieces. Put aside. Take one onion and cut it in half. Drop the halves into the chopper. Give it a whirl. Scoop mince out. Put aside.

3. Take pork loin. Cut 1inch thick vertical slices. Six slices should suffice (3 per serving). If loin is long, leave the remaining piece of meat intact. It can be used to make a small

pork roast. Freeze it if necessary. Place six pork medallions on a plate along with a sprig of fresh rosemary. Put aside.

Final Preparation & Presentation of

Black Olive Canapés
Slice French bread into 4 or 6 pieces (for 2 or 3 canapés each). Spread each slice with cream cheese. Get bowl of puréed olives. Mix paste then top the slices with the spread/pâté. Arrange canapés on a serving dish. Grate lemon zest (if you have a lemon) atop to garnish. Sprinkle a few fresh thyme leaves here and there. Serve.

Amatriciana (Bacon & Onion) Spaghetti
Pull out a large frying pan (sauté pan). Pour 1/4 cup of olive oil inside, along with the minced onion. Turn on heat and allow onion to sauté on a medium/low heat until limp (roughly 10 min). Now add bacon, turn up heat slightly and allow onion and bacon to sauté for 2 to 3 minutes. Add tomatoes and hot pepper flakes. Cover and allow sauce to simmer for 15 min. Taste for salt and pepper.

While sauce is simmering, put a pot of water on the stovetop to boil. When it reaches a rolling boil, add two tablespoons of salt to the water. Add pasta (read directions on packet for cooking time). Remember to drain pasta *al dente.* Before draining pasta pull out a cup of starchy water. Put aside. Drain pasta. Add pasta to sauce and mix. Add 1/2 cup of starchy water and continue to stir spaghetti in sauce until all noodles are coated. Serve immediately.

Grilled Pork Medallions

Heat stovetop grill or barbeque. If you do not have a grill you can use broiler. While waiting for grill to heat, take a bowl and add 1/4 cup of olive oil, fresh rosemary (remove the leaves or thickets from the stem), now drop them in oil. Add green or black peppercorns and allow the seasoned oil (marinade) to sit for a few minutes. Toss pork medallions onto grill, barbeque or slide under broiler. Grill on one side, then the other. Salt and pepper both sides. Remove from heat and place pork on dish. In a small frying pan, heat the herb oil. Place the medallions in the pan for a moment, turning them over so they are flavored with the rosemary/peppercorn oil. Turn off heat. Pull out a serving platter, dress it with Arugula greens, place the medallions atop, pour the warm oil atop meat and greens. Grate lemon zest over the entrée. Serve.

Menu Four: Cream Cheese & Sausage Canapés - Bean & Pasta Soup - Chicken Sautéed in Herbs & Black Olives – Sautéed Spinach

Preparation time: 25 min. Total cooking time: 35-40 min.

Shopping – Ingredients to pick up

Fresh oregano, rosemary, sage and a few bay leaves

One medium white or yellow onion

One garlic bulb

One loaf of French bread

Two Italian sausages

Chicken pieces – 4 thighs with bone (or any other pieces with bone)

One 8 oz package of cream cheese

Bottled or canned white beans (2 – 14.28 oz cans or one 28 oz can)

1 small can of tomato paste

One package of tiny bow pasta or short macaroni noodles

Vegetable broth (granular, liquid or cube) – 6 cups

One small can black olives – not entire can will be used so keep olives for antipasti or make a pâté (recipe in previous menu plan)

Olive oil

1 package of frozen spinach

Advance Preparation

1. Take two sausages and remove minced pork from its casing. Do this by squeezing the pork out into a bowl. Now add half the cream cheese and a spoon (tea size) of fresh thyme or oregano to the sausage. Add a pinch of salt and dash of pepper. Mix pork, herbs and cream cheese into a creamy paste. Cover and set aside. Put in fridge if made ahead of time.

2. Open beans and drain packing water. Drop beans into a pasta strainer (colander). Rinse under tap water for a minute or so to remove packing liquid. Set aside.

3. Get a pot. Add 4 cups of water and two vegetable bouillons or one heaping tbsp. of granular broth. Allow broth to reach a boil. Get another pot (at least 3 quart size). Add three tablespoons of olive oil, two minced garlic cloves and a sprig of fresh rosemary. Turn on heat and allow garlic to sauté for a minute or so in the oil. Toss in beans.

4. Add a dash of pepper and pinch or two of salt. Now add 1cup of hot broth and one tablespoon of tomato paste to beans. Stir. Allow beans to simmer for 15 min while prepping entrée.

5. Take cutting board and knife. Cut and clean chicken, removing as much of the skin as possible. Rinse pieces. Pat dry. Clean board and knife.

6. In a large frying pan (or sauté pan), add three tablespoons of olive oil and a heaping tablespoon of as many of the following herbs as you have around (sage, rosemary, bay leaves, thyme). Toss 1/2 of a white or yellow onion into the food processor or small mincing apparatus along with a clove of garlic. Give it a whirl. Add this mince to the pan. Place the pan on stovetop and turn on heat. Sauté the mince on medium/low heat until the onion is limp (roughly 10 minutes). Now salt and pepper chicken pieces and toss them into pan. Allow them to brown (roughly another 10 to 15 minutes). This means turning them so they become golden on all sides. Now add 1/2 cup of vegetable broth, cover and allow chicken to simmer for 20 minutes. If liquid evaporates quickly, add a bit more broth.

7. Pull spinach from freeze and allow it to thaw. Chop one clove of fresh garlic and put both aside.

Final Preparation & Presentation of

Cream Cheese & Sausage Canapés

Slice 4 to 6 pieces of French bread into rounds. Spread the sausage and cheese mixture made earlier on each slice of bread. Place these canapés on a baking sheet. Drizzle each with olive oil and set aside. Heat the broiler. These canapés should be popped under the broiler for about 3 to 4 minutes just before serving time. Remember: once the sausage turns beige pull canapés from the broiler. Don't over-cook the pork. These canapés are to be creamy not dry. I suggest popping them under the broiler once you have tossed the pasta into the bean soup. That way you will pull them out five minutes before the soup is ready. Being they are finger foods, they can even be served standing as you are stirring the soup.

Bean & Pasta Soup (Pasta A Fagioli)

Once the beans have simmered for 15 to 20 minutes taste for salt and pepper. After seasoning, take a mini primer/hand blender and purée the beans in the pot. Result: a creamy thick soup. Now toss in 2 cups of vegetable broth and put the pot back on the stove. Allow it to reach boiling point. Toss in 2 cups of pasta and allow it to cook in beans and broth. As noodles swell, absorbing the liquid, add a bit more broth when needed. The consistency of the soup shouldn't be too watery or too thick. Ladle soup into bowls, drizzle with a swirl of olive oil, sprinkle a few fresh thyme leaves and serve.

Chicken Sautéed in Herbs & Black Olives - Sautéed Spinach

The chicken should be almost cooked by now (if it has been simmering for 30 minutes or so). Taste for salt but remember you will be adding the black olives in a moment and they are also salty. Being the chicken has been simmering for a while, there probably isn't much liquid left in the pan. If there is, turn up heat and allow some liquid to fire off (evaporate) until you hear a slight crackling sound coming from the pan and the chicken begins to stick to the bottom and sides. Scrape the drippings from pan and add 1/4 cup of vegetable broth and 1/2 cup of black olives. Stir and allow chicken to simmer for 5 more minutes.

Take a small frying pan. Add 2 tablespoons of olive oil and a clove of minced garlic. Sauté garlic until it is lightly colored. Drain excess water from thawed spinach. Toss into pan with a pinch of salt and dash of pepper. Allow greens to heat for 5 minutes or so. The spinach, having been cooked before it was frozen merely needs to be heated with the fresh garlic.

Once the first course, in this case bean soup, has been served. Transfer the chicken onto a platter, cover it with the olives and juices and serve alongside the sautéed spinach and a basket of bread.

Sophomore Year - Setting The Table & Mood

I have no intention of presenting a diagram on how a table should be set for an informal meal. However, there are a few aspects to setting the table European style that I feel are important to know if you are aiming for an authentic Mediterranean dining experience.

Placement: When placing silverware, the knife goes to the right (blade facing the plate) and the fork to the left of your dinner plate. If you are serving soup, the spoon sits to the right of the knife. If you are serving coffee or dessert, the dessert spoon, or fork sits at the head of the dish. The glass should be placed just above the tip of the knife (slightly above the plate). If you intend to serve wine, the wine glass sits alongside the water glass (from right to left – first wine then water). If, a sparkling wine (*spumante*) is to be served, you will place the flute behind the water and wine glasses.

Dishes. Italian meals are served in courses, which means you will have a dinner plate, a low rimmed bowl for pasta or soup, and possibly a salad plate (for antipasto and/or salad at the end of the meal).

The pasta bowl sits on top of the dinner plate, while the antipasto plate usually sits on the low-rimmed bowl. Otherwise, one can sit the antipasto plate on the dinner plate and keep the pasta bowls aside until the antipasto has been served, then replace that plate with the bowl. Napkins are nicely folded and placed on the antipasto plate or bowl.

Once the first course has been enjoyed, remove the bowls, leaving the dinner plate for the entrée and side dish.

Note: Lingering between courses is customary in Italy. So, try to pace your meal, keeping a ten-minute *intervallo* for conversing between courses.

Something to keep in mind: In most restaurants in Italy, bread is brought to the table upon sitting down. But when serving a meal in a Tuscan home, bread is usually brought to the table with the entrée and side dish, unless an antipasto like Italian cold cuts are being served first. Reason being, most Italians, at least Tuscans, rarely eat bread with first courses like pasta or rice.

Setting the Mood. Try Bocelli, Eros Ramazzoti or Laura Pausini as background music. And don't forget the candles.

Menu One: Fried Zucchini Blossoms & Fried Sage Leaves - Spicy Tomato & Herb Pasta - Grilled Provolone & Veggies

Preparation Time: 25 minutes; Cooking and grilling time: 25 minutes

Shopping – Ingredients to pick up

12 zucchini flowers or one long zucchini & one carrot

24 fresh sage leaves (the biggest you can find)

Fresh oregano, basil & rosemary

Breadcrumbs (toss a few break sticks into a chopper for crumbs)

Crusty French bread

One garlic bulb

One lemon

½ cup flour & sparkling water or beer for batter

Olive oil

Red wine vinegar

One 14.28 can of Italian plum tomatoes (no herbs added)

One 1/2 lb package of spaghetti or linguini

Red hot pepper flakes

Italian Provolone (a chunk that can be sliced into four 1 inch rounds)

One egg

One bag of Arugula

2 more long zucchini

1 eggplant (oblong)

¼ cream cheese

Anchovy paste (optional)

Sunflower seed oil (or another frying oil)

Advance Preparation

1. Wash zucchini blossoms and fresh sage. If you couldn't find blossoms (flowers) and bought on long zucchini and a carrot then julienne both carrot and zucchini and put the thin strips aside. Now make a batter with flour, sparkling water (or beer). This batter should be of medium consistency (not watery or too thick). Add salt and pepper and a few fresh thyme leaves to batter and put aside.

2. Chop two cloves of garlic. Set aside. Pull out large sauté pan. Pour in 1/4 cup of olive oil and add minced garlic and

two fresh rosemary sprigs. Allow garlic and herb to sauté for a couple of minutes. Add the can of Italian tomatoes along with red hot pepper flakes. Season with salt. Allow sauce to simmer on medium heat for 15 to 20 minutes. Turn off heat. Cover and set aside until the time comes to make the pasta.

3. Pull out cutting board and chef knife. Rinse the other two zucchini and eggplant. Slice eggplant lengthwise into 1/4 inch slices (you should get about four long slices). Salt slices on both sides. Let veggies sit and sweat for 15 minutes. The salt draws out the acidity. Cut zucchini into long slices.

4. Pull out grill and heat it over burner. Rinse salt from eggplant and pat dry. Grill both eggplant and zucchini until they are line scorched on both sides. Place veggies on cutting board. Slice both into long, thin julienne strips. Arrange strips on a platter. Set aside.

5. Put water in a large pasta pot on the stovetop to heat.

6. Make a vinaigrette: 3/4 cup of olive oil, three tablespoons balsamic vinegar, 1 small garlic clove (minced), salt and pepper to taste. Toss ingredients into blender along with fresh oregano leaves. Blend. Pour dressing into a cup. Set aside. This vinaigrette will keep up to a week.

Final Preparation & Presentation of

Fried Zucchini Blossoms and Fried Sage

Get batter, zucchini blossoms (or julienne zucchini and carrots), and sage, cream cheese and anchovy paste. Now take sage leaves and spread a dollop of cream cheese on one leaf. Add a squirt of anchovy paste (this will give the sage a salty taste... you really cannot taste the anchovy paste). Now cover the leaf with another leaf (like a sandwich). Prepare all leaves (should be 12 couples). Now heat the oil for frying in a pan. Dip sage leaves in batter and drop in oil. Allow them to fry for a minute or so. Do the same with zucchini blossoms. If you have julienne zucchini and carrots, then grab a small bunch (mixed carrots and zucchini) dip the bush in the batter and drop them into the hot oil. Allow them to fry until golden. Place all fried veggies on a paper towel to absorb oil. Transfer to platter. Sprinkle with sea salt and enjoy. These are finger foods so can be served with a glass of wine while still preparing the first course. Or, if served at the table (then place platter in a slightly warm (fanned oven) until ready to serve. This will keep them crisp.

Spicy Tomato & Herb Pasta

When pasta water comes to a rolling boil, toss in two heaping tbsp. of salt and 1/2 a package of spaghetti (3/4 for big eaters). Note the cooking time on package. Pasta should be drained *al dente* so do not overcook. While pasta is cooking, turn heat back on the previously prepared sauce. Take the egg, crack it and allow the whites to slip through your fingers into a cup. Place the yolk in another cup. You will not be using the egg whites so set them aside.

Before draining the *al dente* pasta, collect a cup of hot starchy water from the pot. Toss the strained noodles into the pan of sauce. Drop the yolk and 1/4 cup of the starchy pasta water into the sauce and pasta. Mix, making sure all the noodles are coated with the sauce. You should have a creamy red sauce. Add more water if need be to make sure the noodles are saucy and creamy. Remove pot from heat after one minute, as that is all that is needed to cook yolk and cream up sauce. Serve immediately.

Grilled Provolone & Veggies dressed in a Vinaigrette

Put a griddle/grill on the burner to heat. Slice provolone into 1 inch thick pieces. Rub olive oil on both sides. Sprinkle breadcrumbs atop each slice. Once grill is hot, place the breaded cheese slices on top. Allow slices to heat until a golden crust forms (approx.2 minutes), then turn over and repeat grilling on other side. The cheese begins to slightly melt inside while crust forms outside. Note: If you have a microwave, you can grill the cheese slices ahead of time.

Just cover them until you want to serve. Pop the slices into the microwave for 30 seconds so the cheese melts a bit inside. If you don't have a microwave, I suggest grilling the cheese just before serving. Remove cheese from grill.

Dress a serving platter with a bed of Arugula and place grilled cheese rounds on top. Pull out the platter of grilled vegetables. Chop a bit of fresh basil (if on hand) and sprinkle atop veggies before dressing them with vinaigrette. Place the remaining vinaigrette on the table to dress the Arugula. Serve cheese, veggies and Arugula alongside crusty French bread.

***

Menu Two: Tomatoes Stuffed with Tuna Salad - Savory Shrimp, Zucchini & Basil Pasta - Grilled Salmon Dressed in a Rosemary Vinaigrette

Preparation Time: 25 minutes; Cooking and Grilling Time: 20 minutes

Shopping – Ingredients to pick up

One small can of tuna packed in oil or water

6 ripe Italian plum tomatoes

Fresh oregano, rosemary & basil

One lemon

One medium size farm fresh egg

One bulb of garlic

2 long zucchini

Capers (optional) for stuffed tomatoes

1 dozen medium size shrimp (allow min of 6 shrimp each)

One pkg. lasagna noodles (remember only half a package is needed so check your cupboard for wide noodles before shopping)

Olive oil

Balsamic vinegar

Vegetable bouillon

Two fresh salmon fillets

Two large white potatoes

One loaf of French bread

Advance Preparation

1. Drain water or oil from canned tuna. Toss tuna into a bowl along with 1/2 tbsp of fresh oregano leaves. Set aside.

2. Pull out mini primer or hand blender. Take one egg. Preferably room temperature and not straight from fridge. Crack egg into a tall, jar like, container that the hand blender fits comfortably inside. Cut the lemon in half. Squeeze the juice atop the egg. Pour 1/4 cup of olive oil into the jar as well. Begin pulsing the blender to mix ingredients. Little by little rain more oil into the jar as you pulse the blender. The oil allows the creamy mayo to thicken. Lift the blender up and down while pulsing. Add a pinch or two of salt once mayo thickens. You can even toss in a few fresh herbs (oregano, thyme or basil) at the end as well. Taste mayo for salt and lemon. Add if need be. Note: if you take the egg directly from the fridge and toss it in the jar, the coldness of the egg may not allow the oil and egg to amalgamate. Thus, allow

egg to sit out at least 1/2 an hour before making mayo. Pour mayo into a bowl, cover with wrap and put in fridge. It tends to thicken more when left to sit in fridge.

3. Take 2 Italian plum tomatoes. Slice them in half (length-wise). Scoop out the inner pulp. Toss the pulp into the bowl with the tuna, fresh herbs, salt and pepper. Put the 4 hollow tomato shells on a plate. Mix the tuna and chopped tomato pulp with 2 tablespoons of homemade mayo. For those who didn't venture out to make mayo, a good store bought mayo can also be used. Fill the tomato 'boats' with the tuna salad. Cover and put into fridge.

4. Take zucchini. Slice lengthwise into long strips. Gather the strips and slice lengthwise again. This gives you numerous julienne strips. Put aside.

5. Take the remaining 4 Italian plum tomatoes and dice them.

6. Mince two garlic cloves. Put both tomatoes and garlic aside.

7. Take at least 10 fresh basil leaves. Gather them in one hand, bend the lot in half, and slice basil into 1/8 inch strips on a cutting board. This gives you julienne basil strips.

8. Clean shrimp (if need be) by removing outer skin/shell.

9. Boil potatoes in a pot of water for 20 minutes or until they are soft but not mushy. Allow them to cool before peeling.

10. Pour 1/4 a cup of olive oil into a bowl. Add green peppercorns, one tablespoon of fresh rosemary leaves and a clove of minced garlic. Allow marinade to sit for 30 minutes.

Final Preparation & Presentation of

Tomatoes Stuffed with Tuna & Homemade Mayonnaise
Pull the stuffed tomatoes from the fridge. Place them atop a bed of lettuce greens. Grate lemon zest atop. Decorate each stuffed tomato with a caper or two. Serve alongside a basket of French bread.

Shrimp, Zucchini & Basil Pasta
Fill pasta pot with water and heat. In the meantime, take a big sauté pan or frying pan. Pour 1/4 cup of olive oil inside. Add minced garlic and sauté for a couple of minutes. Toss in the julienne zucchini. Stir fry for 5 min in oil and garlic before tossing in diced tomatoes. Add 1/4 cup of vegetable broth if needed, then sauté veggies for 10-12 minutes. Lower heat and toss in shrimp. Allow shrimp to cook with veggies for 2 minutes (no longer). They should be PALE pink. Cover pot and turn off heat. Now pasta water should almost have reached a rolling boil. If so, add two tablespoons of salt and toss in linguini noodles. Check cooking time (probably about 9 to 11 minutes). When noodles are *al dente* (even a minute before) strain them. Remember to collect a cup of the starchy pasta water from

the pot to put aside. Toss strained noodles into sauté pan along with veggies and shrimp. Turn on heat to high. Add half of the starchy water and begin mixing noodles into sauce. Now toss the fresh basil into the sauté. Stir until all the noodles are coated with sauce. Serve.

Grilled Salmon & Potatoes

Pull broiling pan out from oven. Dress with parchment paper or aluminum foil. Place the two fillets on the foil or paper. Drizzle the rosemary scented oil atop each fillet. Make sure some of the rosemary leaves and green peppercorns fall onto the fish. Sprinkle salt and pepper atop. Stick under broiler for 3 to 4 minutes. In the meantime, collect the two parboiled potatoes. Slice them into 1/8 inch slices. Place slices on a serving dish. Salt and pepper them and drizzle them with the rosemary and green peppercorn oil. Now turn salmon fillets over and allow them a couple more minutes under the broiler. They should be ready in no more than 5-6 minutes (total broiling time). Do not overcook. They should be light pink and flaky when cut into. Place them on the serving dish alongside the potatoes. If you ventured to make the tasty homemade mayo, scoop a spoon alongside each fillet. If not, drizzle an idea of the rosemary and green peppercorn oil atop. Serve along with French bread.
An Idea! Slice 1/2 a loaf of French bread lengthwise. Brush it with the rosemary oil and pop it under the grill once the fish has been removed. Pull it out when the sides and top are toasty golden. Slice and serve.

Menu Three: Marinated Mushroom & Parmesan Canapés - Porcini Mushroom Pasta - Creamy Lemon Chicken

Prep time: 25 min; Cooking time: 20 min Marinating: 60 min

Shopping – Ingredients to pick up

One dozen good sized white champignon mushrooms

2 lemons

A bunch of fresh Italian parsley

Parmesan cheese shavings (either grated strips or a piece that can be shaved into strips)

Hot chili flakes or pepper

Olive oil

All purpose flour (used to coat chicken breast)

One package of linguini (remember only half is need so check cupboard for an open package before buying)

One package of dried Italian porcini mushrooms

Two sprigs of fresh thyme

4 or 5 Italian plum tomatoes

One bulb of garlic

A vegetable bouillon, granular or stock broth

One chicken breast

One egg

Fresh sage

One loaf of French bread

Salad fixings

Advance Preparation

1. Wash mushrooms. Remove stem from cap. Slice mushrooms lengthwise and toss pieces into a bowl.

2. Cut the lemons in half. Squeeze juice out with hand juicer or with a fork. Should be at least 1/2 a cup of juice. Set both juice and rinds aside.

3. Pour half the lemon juice over the mushrooms. The rest goes into the chicken later.

4. Chop fresh parsley and two garlic cloves. Put mince aside.

5. Add 2 tbsp of mince to the mushrooms. Sprinkle salt and chili pepper flakes (spicy is optional) atop the mushrooms. Then cover them with plastic wrap and put them in a cool place – even in the fridge. The mushrooms can be prepared up to four hours ahead of dinner.

6. Open package of dried porcini mushrooms and drop them into a bowl of warm water. Allow them to soak for at least 30 minutes.

7. Pull out cutting board. Dice plum tomatoes. Put aside.

8. Wash chicken breast. Pat dry. Divide breast into two halves. Open each half by slicing through the breast horizontally without slicing completely through. Salt and pepper the breast halves. Coat breasts with flour and put aside.

9. Heat one cup of vegetable broth.

10. And now for the final preparations...

Final Preparation & Presentation of

Marinated Mushroom & Parmesan Canapés

Remove the marinated mushrooms from the fridge. Uncover and mix around. They should have expelled enough water to where they are swimming in a lemony marinade. Take half a loaf of French bread and cut 4 to 6 slices (2 or 3 canapés per person). Spoon mushrooms, along with marinade onto each slice. Drizzle the canapés with olive oil. Grate Parmesan shavings atop. Serve.

Porcini Mushroom Pasta

Take a sauté pan. Add 1/4 cup of olive oil and 2 tbsp. of the already minced garlic and parsley. Sauté minced garlic for a minute. Squeeze the water from the mushrooms but DO NOT disregard liquid. Toss the mushrooms into sauté. Add a bit of the soaking water and allow the mushrooms to simmer for 15 minutes. Salt and pepper to taste. After 15 to 20 minutes add diced tomatoes, along with a 1/4cup vegetable broth. Allow the lot to simmer for another 10 to 15 minutes. So that some of the liquid evaporates while the tomatoes and mushrooms are stewing.

Fill a pasta pot with water. When water comes to a rolling boil, toss in two tablespoons of salt and half a pack of penne pasta. Allow pasta to cook to the *al dente* stage (9 to 11 minutes depending on brand). Before straining pasta, collect a cup of the starchy pasta water.

Toss pasta into mushroom sauté. Add a bit of the starchy water to cream up the sauce if need be. Mix and garnish the pasta with Parmesan shavings. Serve.

Creamy Lemon Chicken
Heat 3 tablespoons of olive oil in a medium sized frying pan (one where chicken breasts fit comfortably). Place the flour dusted breasts in the oil and allow them to brown on both sides (about 3 min per side) Toss in a tablespoon of the garlic and parsley mince. Add 1/4 cup of vegetable broth, then cover with lid and allow chicken to simmer for 10 minutes.

In the meantime take one egg. Crack it, allowing the egg white to slip through your fingers into a glass. Collect the yolk. We will not be using the egg white so put it in the fridge to make an egg white omelet the next morning. Drop the egg yolk into the lemon juice. There should be about 1/4 cup leftover from before. Mix the juice and the egg yolk with a fork for a minute or so. Add a pinch of salt.

Uncover the chicken breasts, which should be cooked, pour the egg and lemon juice into the pan and stir with a wooden spoon. The lemon and egg will thicken into a creamy sauce. If too thick, add a bit of vegetable broth. Allow chicken to simmer in the sauce for another minute. Turn heat off and transfer breasts to a platter. Now pour the creamy lemon sauce atop and serve alongside warm bread and a mixed green salad dressed in oil and vinegar.

Menu Four: Blue Cheese & Walnut Canapés - *Nudi* (Spinach & Ricotta Ravioli) dressed in Butter & Sage - Artichoke & Sausage *Frittata*

Preparation Time: 25 minutes   Cooking Time: 20 -25 minutes

Shopping – Ingredients to pick up

One fresh rose (red, pink or yellow)

1/4 lb. of creamy blue cheese

Half a dozen walnuts (to shell or shelled)

One small package of frozen spinach

One small container of Ricotta cheese

Fresh sage (at least a dozen leaves)

Butter (preferably non-salted)

2 sausage links

6 eggs

2 fresh artichokes OR a small package of frozen artichoke hearts

One small onion (white or yellow)

Fresh Thyme

Nutmeg

Vegetable broth (granular, bouillon or stock) – roughly 1/2 a cup

Parmesan cheese (grated)

One loaf of French bread

Sugar (preferably very fine sugar – brown or white.

Milk (only half a cup is needed)

Salad fixings

Advance Preparation

1. Take half the loaf of bread and slice it into 8 round canapés. Pop them under the broiler or in a toaster.

2. Shell walnuts. Collect the meaty halves. Put aside

3. Thaw spinach

4. Clean fresh artichokes by removing hard outer leaves and choke. Place in water with a tbsp of lemon juice. OR thaw frozen artichoke hearts if fresh are not available.

5. Mince onion

6. Remove minced pork from sausage casing and place in bowl along with a sprig of fresh thyme.

7. Take one of the 6 eggs. Crack it and divide the white from the yolk. Put yolk aside.

8. Whisk the white until foamy. Pour 1/2 a cup of sugar onto a small dessert dish.

9. Take the rose. Remove its pedals very carefully so they do not rip. Dip each pedal in the egg white (coating the entire pedal) then dip into the sugar (coating both sides).

10. Lay the pedals on a rack to air dry for at least an hour. The rack from inside the stove usually works well.

11. Place a large pot of water on the stovetop to heat.

Final Preparation & Presentation of

Blue Cheese & Walnut Canapés

Collect the toasted canapés and spread a generous amount of creamy Gorgonzola cheese atop each round. Place a walnut half on each toast. Place canapés on a small serving platter and surround them with the sugar coated rose pedals. Sprinkle the lot with fresh thyme leaves and serve. Pair these tasty canapés with a glass of sparkling white wine.

Gnocchi (Spinach & Ricotta Ravioli) dressed in Butter & Sage

Collect the thawed spinach. Squeeze out excess water and toss spinach into a mixing bowl. Add approximately 2 cups of fresh ricotta cheese, 1/4 cup of Parmesan cheese, a pinch of salt, a dash of pepper and a dash of nutmeg. Crack one egg and toss it into the bowl. Mix ingredients thoroughly. Now form individual balls about the size of walnuts. Gently roll balls in a bit of flour and put aside.

Take a large bowl, one that sits comfortably atop the pot of boiling water. Drop sage leaves inside the bowl adding 3 tablespoons of sweet butter, a pinch of pepper and a dash of nutmeg. Put bowl on top of pasta pot. When butter has melted from the steam surging in the pot below, remove the bowl. Add two tablespoons of sea salt to the water and begin to drop the 'nudi' (naked ravioli) balls into the boiling water. Have a perforated spoon (one with holes in it) ready to scoop up the 'nudi' or gnocchi once they float to the top of the surface of the boiling water. Allow them to float for a minute before scooping them up and placing them into the melted butter and sage. When all the gnocchi have been dressed, sprinkle the lot with Parmesan cheese and serve.

Artichoke and Sausage Frittata

Take artichokes, along with the minced onion and toss both into a frying pan along with 2 tablespoons of olive oil. Sauté for 3 or 4 minutes or until onion goes limp. Make a cup of vegetable broth using one-cup water and one tbsp. granular broth or a bouillon cube. Add a teaspoon of fresh thyme leave, season with salt and pepper. Cover and allow artichokes to simmer for 15 min or until they are tender and limp. If, broth evaporates, add a bit more. Once artichokes are tender but still holding their own, toss in sausage meat. Turn up heat and allow meat to cook with artichokes until pork becomes light beige and the liquid from artichokes has evaporated. Turn off heat.

In a bowl, crack 4 eggs, whisk together with 1/2 cup of milk and 1/2 cup of Parmesan cheese. Take a baking pan. Grease it with olive oil. Do this by pouring a bit of oil in the pan, rubbing it around bottom and sides with a napkin. Pour artichoke and sausage mix into the pan. Cover it with the egg batter and slip the pan into a 350° preheated oven for fifteen minutes. Remove when frittata is golden in color. Slice and serve alongside a crisp salad dressed in olive oil and vinegar and warm bread.

Junior Year - Let's Talk Wine

Italians, having grown up with bottles, carafes and flasks of wine on dinner tables nightly, consider this alcoholic beverage part of their dining ritual. For this reason, the majority of young Italians (though times are changing) enjoy wine as a complement to a meal rather than a means of getting drunk. In fact many young Italians are intolerant of those friends or acquaintances that practice binge drinking to merely get a buzz. This, to many, is unacceptable behavior often deemed stupid. Many times such behavior can put the drunken culprit on a fast track to being excluded from groups and parties. It seems the older these young Italians get, the more intolerant they become with those whose drinking habits are considered out of their norm – i.e. binge-drinking on weekends. That's not to say these young Italians aren't ordering drinks when they go to discos or clubs on the weekends. They are. It's customary to see groups of five or six young adults sharing a bottle of champagne at clubs and discos. You see, like their eating habits, most young Italians still drink in moderation. The majority of these young adults haven't embraced the binge-drinking phenomenon, however, globalization is straining the 'good drinking habits' of the fourteen to eighteen year old group. But on the whole, ethnicity continues to trump globalization, at least for now.

When enjoyed in moderation and coupled with food, wine can easily be incorporated into a healthy life style. Pairing wine with a meal can make for an evening of endless delights. By learning to enjoy wine one is well on the way to becoming a *buongustaio*. Appreciating good wine with a meal means succumbing to the pleasures of Italian dining. But to appreciate this 'nectar of the gods,' one must understand just how it is born.

Below is an excerpt from my book, Zucchini Blossoms – A Culinary Memoir & Recipes from Tuscany. It is my hope that this information may give insight as to why Italians not only love their wines but respect them as well.

***

Seasons in a Tuscan Vineyard

What makes a wine fit for the gods? Apart from **sun, stone, silence, solitude and drought**- nature's ingredients, it takes a knowledgeable alchemist, one who lovingly cares for his/her vines season after season so that these vines are able to produce nothing short of a good, if not great, wine.

Summer marks the beginning (and end) of the grape harvest. Though there is no set day a winemaker says, *"andiamo a vendemmiare"* (let's go pick), this decision to head for the vineyard with shears in hand is not taken lightly. Every winemaker knows that picking grapes too early or too late can mean the difference between a mediocre, good or even great wine. But when is it too early or too late? Picking early, before grapes have reached complete maturity, can yield a lighter wine. Although good, chances are it won't be great. Waiting that extra week to ten days may allow grapes to completely mature on the vine, which could make a world of difference. But what if it rains? Winemakers worldwide gamble on the weather and Tuscan growers are no different. This unwanted gift from Mother Nature could ruin a harvest and a potentially great vintage year. So what is a winemaker to do when late August rolls around? He or she does nothing more than listen to weather reports before calling in their faithful pickers. Ultimately, it's the forecast that decides when baskets and shears fill the vineyards.

And when this time comes not just anyone is asked to join the *vendemmia* (grape harvest), and for good reason. No winemaker wants impatient pickers, those who grab clusters or rip them from the vine, possibly damaging the grapes. Nor do growers want untrained pickers who pick indiscriminately. These novice workers tend to collect damaged and mildewed clusters along with the plump, juicy ones. Thus, it's easily understood why grape growers are so selective when hiring their picking crew. For nothing short of the best clusters must make their way to the *cantina.* The sacred place where the alchemy of grapes to wine begins.

Autumn silently creeps in, stripping Tuscan vineyards of their lush attire. It's the season of changing wardrobes. It's when leaves quickly turn from vibrant green to crimson, to yellow before dropping to the ground on the slightest disturbance. Within a matter of weeks Tuscan vineyards are completely naked, their vines standing motionless atop a melancholy carpet of leaves. But beneath the soil of these vines their roots are very much alive. Much like groundhogs, they are preparing for a long winter's nap.

Winter vineyards, with their gnarled and naked branches, are certainly no photographer's dream. Accept on those mornings when a low-lying fog sails across the rolling hills and vineyards of Tuscany like a lone schooner. These seemingly abandoned vines create a different picture to the experienced grape grower. As winter vineyards represent the end of a hopefully award-winning season and the beginning of a new wine adventure.

Spring is one of nature's busiest seasons. As vineyards are bathed in afternoon showers, buds emerge from their newly born shoots to look down upon red poppies, blue bells and yellow broom. These are the flowers that dress Tuscan fields in their most colorful attire.

Not only blessed with this fertile terrain, Tuscany is also graced with an ideal climate for grape growing. But despite these attributes, it still takes the constant attention of dedicated growers to protect vineyards from the season's most deadly enemy: spring fungus. If fungus attacks the newly formed clusters the outcome could be devastating. The immature fruit could dry up before summer. To avoid this unwelcome scenario, winemakers set out to *ramare* (spray) every vine in hopes of protecting the grapes. But which type of grape is found on Tuscan vines?

To the inexperienced eye, recognizing a grape's type is not easy. But for grape growers it's a piece of cake. A simple glance at the leaves will reveal what type of cluster is forming on any given vine. Tuscan vineyards are predominantly home to *Sangiovese* , *Malvasino Bianco, Trebbiano,* and *Colorino* grapes. Although not as frequent, *Cabernet* and *Merlot* grapes are also grown in Tuscany, especially near *Bolgheri,* the Super Tuscan wine region.

But let's take a closer look at the clusters. The experienced grower knows that full clusters, with fruit pushing against one another, although seemingly the best ones for wine making, are not the ones that ultimately produce fine wines. It's the clusters with ample space between its fruit that are actually the better ones. Why? Well, when those spring showers bathe vineyards, it's the open clusters that have the advantage of drying out in *Eostre's* (the goddess of spring) welcome breeze. The close-knit clusters don't share this advantage. Thus, making it easier for the latter to develop *bunch-rot.* This leaves the immature, damp grapes to rot on the vine, together with their too close for comfort neighbors.

Now that we've gone full circle, *summer* rolls in once more. And with summer comes Mother Nature who gives us a lesson in just how she provides since most vineyards in Tuscany have no irrigation systems (there are no tubes lining the soil). So how do grapes resist summer's heat and a lack of water? How do they thrive and survive? The simple truth is the vines do feel stressed, especially when those hot summer days turn into weeks. But remember, *sun, sand, stone, solitude* and *drought*? When vineyards feel stressed from a lack of moisture and heat, vines are prompted to change their hormonal condition. They immediately stop producing leaves while the existing ones take on a new herculean role. During the hottest hours of the day, these leaves transform themselves into verdant sun umbrellas, taking on the formidable task of protecting clusters from the heat by creating a perfect canopy for their fruit. Then, during the cooler hours, they change once more. This time they twist and turn, transforming themselves into solar panels that catch the sun's mildest rays. Thus, allowing the just amount of warmth to be cast on the maturing fruit. One might say that nature has taught her children well, even if the industrious wine maker is never far away. For it takes both man and nature to maintain this perfect circle of life. A cycle that enables Italian winemakers to produce, good, great and even vintage wines year after year.

Menu One: Shrimp & Bean Salad - Crabmeat Pasta in Creamy Lemon Sauce - Jumbo Shrimp Sautéed Herbs

Preparation time: 25 minutes; Cooking Time: 10 – 12 minutes

Shopping – Ingredients to pick up

1/2 lb. Baby shrimp (fresh, pre-cooked or even frozen)

1 -14.28 oz. bottle or can of white beans

Fresh chives

One garlic bulb

Olive oil

1 small can of crabmeat

One egg

Three lemons

A bunch of Italian parsley

One sprig of thyme

1 pack of linguini pasta (half a pack is needed so check cupboard)

8 - 10 jumbo prawns

Red hot pepper flakes

Salt & pepper

Vegetable broth (bouillon, granular or stock)

One loaf of French bread

Salad Greens

Advance Preparation

1. Open can of beans, drain liquid, rinse beans thoroughly to remove packing liquid. Toss beans into serving bowl.

2. Clean or thaw baby shrimp. Rinse, pat dry and toss into bowl. Cover with plastic wrap and put in fridge until ready to dress.

3. Open Crab meat

4. Mince two garlic cloves. Set aside.

5. Mince a tbsp. worth of fresh chives. Set aside.

6. Chop parsley (at least 3 tablespoons) Set aside.

7. Juice one lemon. Put aside but keep the halves to zest with.

8. Slice the second lemon into 1/8inch slices. Set aside.

9. Clean jumbo shrimp by removing the long black thread found running down the spine. Set aside.

10. Fill pasta pot with water and put on the stove to boil.

Final Preparation & Presentation of

Shrimp & Bean Salad
Pull the beans and shrimp from fridge. In a pot of boiling water with one tbsp. of salt, drop in shrimp for 30 seconds or until they turn pink. Scoop out with a perforated spoon. Toss in a bowl. Now take the beans, rinse all packing water and drop in the boiling water for 30 seconds, scoop out with perforated spoon and toss into bowl with shrimp. Prepare vinaigrette (2 tablespoons of olive oil, the juice of half a lemon, salt and pepper). Dress the salad and toss in the chives. Mix. Taste for salt and pepper. Serve alongside a basket of warm French bread.

Crab Pasta in Creamy Lemon Sauce
Pull out a large frying or sauté pan. Add 1/4 cup of olive oil and half of the minced garlic and sauté garlic for one minute. Add crabmeat and its juice. Now add 1/4cup vegetable broth (make it from stock or bouillon). Allow the crabmeat to simmer in the liquid for 10 minutes. Toss in half the parsley. Turn off heat and cover. There

should still be a bit of liquid in the pan. IF not, add a bit more vegetable broth and allow crab to simmer a few more minutes.

Now take the egg. Crack it and allow the whites to slip through your fingers and into a cup. Toss the yolk into another cup. Put both aside for a moment. You will not be using the whites. IDEA--- make an egg white omelet for breakfast. Back to the pasta dish... Put pot of water on to boil (4-5 quarts). When water reaches a rolling boil toss in two tablespoons of salt and then the pasta (making sure to read the cooking time on the package so that you drain the pasta *al dente*). Before draining the pasta, remember to collect a cup of the starchy pasta water. Now let the noodles slide into the pan of crabmeat, turn on the heat, toss in the egg yolk, the juice of 1/2 a lemon and 1/4 cup of the hot starchy water. Mix pasta into sauce for a minute (no longer). Result: a creamy crab sauce. Add a bit more of the hot starchy water if noodles are sticking together or seem dry. Transfer pasta to a serving platter. Sprinkle with minced parsley. Serve.

Jumbo Prawns Sautéed in Lemon & Herbs

In a large frying pan, add 3 tablespoon of olive oil, one minced garlic clove and a pinch of red hot pepper flakes. Allow garlic to sauté in oil for a minute. Slice a lemon into thin slices (5 or 6). Toss the slices, rind and all, into the pan with the shrimp. Add a bit of chopped parsley. Add a 1/4cup vegetable broth. Turn up flame to high and allow the liquid to evaporate for about 2 minutes. In the meantime, pull out a serving platter and dress it with salad greens. Once shrimp has turned light pink (it shouldn't take more than 3 minutes – 4 at the most) place the crustaceans atop the greens and dress the lot with the dripping in the pan. Sprinkle with sea salt and place the sautéed lemon slices on top. Serve alongside French bread.

Menu Two: *Bruschetta* - Pesto Pasta Bake – Ricotta Stuffed Eggplant in Tomato Sauce
Preparation Time: 35 mins; Cooking and baking time: 25 min

Shopping – Ingredients to pick up

1 loaf Italian or French bread (preferably hard crusted)

A small basket of Italian cherry or plum tomatoes

1 garlic bulb

Fresh oregano

One small white onion

One large bunch of fresh basil

One small bag of pine nuts or half a dozen walnuts

Parmesan cheese (preferably grated) – 1 cup total

Olive oil

2 oval shaped eggplants (aubergines)

1 pint of ricotta cheese

One 14.28 oz. can of Italian plum tomatoes

One package of large bow shaped noodles

Flour – 1/4 cup

Butter -3 tablespoons

Milk (1/2 a quart)

Nutmeg

Sunflower seed oil (optional for frying eggplant instead of grilling)

Hot chili pepper flakes

Salad fixings

Advance Preparation

1. Slice half the loaf of bread into 1/2inch canapés (at least 6 rounds). Toast and put aside.

2. Dice enough tomatoes to fill 1 1/2 cups. Toss into bowl. Chop and sprinkle fresh oregano leaves atop the tomatoes.

3. Mince 1/2 a white onion (small onion). Add to tomatoes and oregano. Dress with 3 tablespoons of olive oil. Stir. Cover and put aside.

4. Pull out a medium size saucepan. Melt 3 tablespoons butter. Add 1/4 cup of flour and a pinch of nutmeg. Stir over low heat until the flour and butter amalgamate, creating a roux (a thickening substance). Now slowing add milk (preferably room temperature and not directly from fridge) and stir. Continue stirring flour, butter and milk until it begins to bubble, forming a thick, creamy white sauce. Add more milk if sauce is too thick, a bit more flour if it's too watery. When ready, (usually 8-10 minutes) sauce should be of a medium consistency. Add a pinch of salt, dash of white pepper (black will do if no white is on hand) and a pinch of nutmet. Cover and set aside.

5. Pull out blender or mini primer. Blend the following: one heap of fresh basil leaves (at least 2 cups packed in), 1/3 cup of pine nuts or walnuts; 1/2 cup of grated parmesan cheese (Reggiano or Romano will also do); 1/2 cup extra vir-gin olive oil; 1 garlic clove; salt and pepper to taste. Add a bit more oil if consistency is too dense. This recipe yields one good size cup of aromatic pesto. Set aside. Clean blender and put it away.

6. Put a pot (4-5 qt.) of water on the stovetop to heat.

7. Slice eggplant lengthwise. You should get 5 slices per aubergine (eggplant). Sprinkle salt on each slice and let stand for 10 mins. The salt will draw out the acidity. Rinse salt off eggplant and pat dry.

8. Now, if you prefer grilling the eggplant then grill each slice on a stovetop grill or in the broiler. If, on the other hand, you prefer frying then dip each in flour and fry in sunflower seed oil. Remove eggplant from skillet when they are golden on each side. Allow them to drain on paper towels. Whether grilling or frying. Once ready. Place on platter and set aside for a moment.

9. Mince two garlic cloves.

10. Take a medium sized saucepan. Add 1/4 cup of olive oil and the minced garlic. Allow to sauté for a minute or so. Toss in Italian plum tomatoes (make sure to drain the watery liquid from the can). Add fresh oregano (a tablespoon of chopped leaves) Taste for salt. Allow sauce to simmer for 20 minutes. Turn off heat.

11. Pre-heat oven to 350° F. or 180 c.

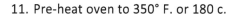

Final Preparation & Presentation

Bruschetta

Collect the bowl of seasoned tomatoes. Place toasted bread canapés on a serving tray. Rub a hint of fresh garlic over each slice. Sprinkle the slices with salt. Now scoop a heaping tablespoon of the marinated tomatoes on top. Drizzle with olive oil and serve.

Pesto Pasta Bake

By now your pasta water should have come to a rolling boil. Toss in two tablespoons of salt and a 1/2 lb. of pasta. Allow pasta to cook for at least 7 or 8 minutes (roughly 3 minutes under its complete cooking stage). Read cooking time on the package. Drain pasta (remember to keep a cup of the hot starchy pasta water aside) then line a baking dish with the pasta noodles. Collect the pre-made pesto. Pour it onto the noodles, along with 1/4 of the hot starchy water. Mix around until all the noodles are coated with the pesto. Fetch the pan of white sauce. If it has been sitting for a while it may have thickened. If so, turn the heat on under the sauce and add a bit of the starchy water. Stir and allow it to heat up again. Once hot and creamy, pour it over the noodles so they are covered in a blanket of white. Sprinkle Parmesan cheese on top. Cover with foil and pop into the oven for 20 minutes. Remove foil for the last five minutes. This allows the top to take on a light golden color while the sauce bubbles between the noodles and pesto. Serve.

Stuffed Eggplant in Spicy Tomato Sauce

Pull out another baking dish. Take grilled or fried eggplant. Fetch ricotta from the fridge. Empty into mixing bowl. Add a bit of salt, pepper and oregano to ricotta. Mix. Now spoon one tablespoon of ricotta atop each slice of eggplant, spreading it with the bottom of the spoon. Roll each stuffed slice and line stuffed eggplant in a pre-greased baking dish. Make sure rolls fit snuggly in the baking pan. Now cover these cheese/veggie rolls with the spicy tomato sauce previously made. Make sure all the rolls are covered and the sauce seeps between each roll. Sprinkle with salt, pepper and Parmesan cheese. Cover eggplant with foil and pop in the oven for 15 min. Remove the foil and allow casserole to bake uncovered for another 10 minutes, allowing for a slightly crusty surface. Serve atop a bed of greens.

Menu Three: Stuffed Mushrooms - Grilled Meat/Vegetable Kabobs & Herb Baked Potatoes

Preparation time: 30 min; Baking & grilling time 30 min

Shopping – Ingredients to pick up

Half a dozen mushrooms with large caps (white or brown)

One small package of frozen spinach

One small white onion & one clove of garlic

Two Italian sausage links

Grated Parmesan cheese (1/2 cup)

One egg

One large chicken breast or piece of pork loin

One large zucchini (or two smaller ones)

One yellow, green or red bell pepper

One loaf of French or Italian bread

4 Italian plum tomatoes (not fully ripe)

Two large baking potatoes

Fresh rosemary, oregano, thyme & olive oil

Advance Preparation

1. Clean mushrooms by removing stems and cleaning under cap allowing mushrooms to be stuffed easily.

2. Dice stems and pieces you scraped from under the cap. Toss in bowl. Put aside for a moment.

3. Thaw and/or boil spinach if it's not already precooked. Drain excess water. Toss spinach into the diced mushroom stems. Salt and pepper the lot. Add 1/4cup Parmesan cheese and a teaspoon of fresh oregano. Set aside.

4. Cut onion in half. Mince one half in a chopper. Slice the other half into pieces for the kabob.

5. Sauté the minced onion in 1 tbsp. olive oil for two minutes. Now toss onion into the spinach/mushroom mix.

6. Take the Italian sausages. Squeeze the pork out of the skin. Drop it into the spinach mixture.

7. Crack the egg inside the spinach mixture. Add 3 tbsp. of Parmesan cheese. Mix ingredients with hands.

8. Sprinkle the lot with a bit more salt and pepper. Now stuff each mushroom cap with the mixture. Making sure to stuff over the brim of each cap. Place the mushrooms snuggly inside a small baking dish. Drizzle olive oil atop. Cover with

foil and put aside. You will certainly have left over stuffing, as this is enough to stuff at least half a dozen more mushrooms, if not more. Put remaining stuffing in the fridge. It is a great base for a frittata (Italian omelet). It will keep a day or two.

9. Preheat oven to 400°F or 200°C

10. Pull out chopping block and chef knife.

11. Wash and pat dry chicken breast or take out pork loin. Cut selected meat (or meats) into cubed, bite size pieces.

12. Take zucchini. Wash and slice into 1inch circles. Do the same with the yellow, green or red bell pepper.

13. Slice half the French bread into 1 1/2 inch rounds.

14. Toss meat cubes, zucchini, pepper and sliced onion into a big bowl. Drizzle the lot with olive oil. Sprinkle with salt, pepper and fresh thyme leaves. Mix. Make sure the ingredients are coated with the oil and herb.

15. Now prepare meat, veggies and bread on a kabob stick, alternating ingredients (i.e. one piece of meat, one vegetable and a slice of bread –repeat). If, you ended up buying a package of sausage for the mushrooms and still have one or two links, cut them into 1 1/2 inch pieces and add them to

the kabob stick. If you have fresh bay leaves growing in the garden, pull a few and stick them on the kabob as well. Set aside kabobs until time to grill or broil them.

16. Peel the potatoes. Cut them into bite size cubes. Place them on a baking pan lined with parchment paper, drizzle with olive oil and sprinkle fresh rosemary, salt and pepper atop. Mix herbs and oil into potatoes with hands. Cover and wait until it's time to pop them in the oven.

Final Preparation & Presentation

Stuffed Mushrooms

The oven should now be preheated to 400°. Pop the mushrooms on the top shelf. They should be covered with foil; on the lower shelf pop in the potatoes (uncovered). The mushrooms should be covered for the first 20 minutes. After which, remove the foil and allow them bake for 10 minutes longer. If mushrooms need to be basted with veggie broth to keep them moist, do so. I would check the potatoes to make sure they are baking evenly at this time as well. Pull them out and mix them up again before returning them to oven to finish baking. The mushrooms should be ready to pull from the oven in roughly 30 minutes. NOTE: all ovens are different so check periodically. Once mushrooms have shrunken to 3/4 their original size and the stuffing is bubbling, they are ready. Remove baking pan from oven.

Allow mushrooms to cool for a few minutes before placing them on a serving tray. Cover them with their own juices and drippings. Serve mushrooms warm, alongside French bread.

Grilled Meat/Vegetable Kabobs & Herb Baked Potatoes

Once you have removed the mushrooms from the oven. Check the potatoes again, turning them over allowing them to get golden on all sides. If you are grilling the kabobs on an outside grill then flare up the heat or coals. If, on the other hand, you are broiling the kabobs in the oven then line them on a rack that has been set atop a baking pan. Turn on the grill, but not before removing the potatoes and covering them. Pop the kebobs under the broiler and allow them to sizzle on both sides. It is good to have a bowl of water with a tbsp. of oil, a dash of pepper and salt added to it, near the oven or barbeque. If you have a fresh rosemary sprig on hand, dip it inside the oily water and brush the kabobs as they grill or broil. This keeps them moist as well as keeping the bread from burning around the edges. If you don't have rosemary on hand, use a long handled spoon to baste kabobs. When the kabobs are golden, remove them from the grill or from under the broiler and place them on a serving platter. Some chefs prefer to remove the meat and vegetable from the sticks before serving, others serve individual kabobs alongside the potatoes.

Menu Four: *Carbonara* Pasta- Arista (Pork Loin Roast) - Beans cooked in Tomato & Sage

Preparation time: 20 min   Cooking & baking time: 40 min

Shopping – What to pick up

Four slabs of bacon (preferably cured and not smoked)

Two eggs (yolks only) or pasteurized egg yolks

One small package of spaghetti (only 1/2 a lb. is needed)

Heavy cream (1/4 cup is needed)

Parmesan cheese (grated)- 1/2 cup is needed

A pinch of nutmeg

A pinch of white pepper

A sprig of fresh thyme

1lb boneless pork loin roast (if more than a pound it's OK because this roast makes great leftovers)

Fresh rosemary

1 bulb garlic

One bunch of fresh sage

3 – 4 Italian plum tomatoes

2 - 14.28 oz cans of white beans

Olive oil

Salt & pepper

Vegetable broth (bouillon, granular or stock)

One loaf of Fresh or Italian bread

Advance Preparation

1. Take out cutting board and chef's knife. Slice bacon into dice size pieces. Put aside.

2. Divide egg whites from yolks. Put the whites back in the fridge. Great for egg white omelet. Pour the yolks in a bowl.

3. Add the Parmesan cheese – 1/2 cup to yolks, 1/4 cup of heavy cream, a pinch of nutmeg and a dash of pepper. Mix and set aside.

4. Fill pot (4-5 qt) with water and put on burner to heat.

5. Take pork loin. Pork 4 or 5 small holes here and there with a knife.

6. Take fresh rosemary sprig. Remove the leaves. Toss them in the food processor along with 2 cloves of fresh garlic. Give it a whirl. Now add a tablespoon of salt to the mince and fill the holes in the pork with the mince.

7. Get a piece of kitchen string (white string or even heavy thread). Tie the roast to keep it compact. Just wrap string around roast (keep it taut) and tie. Now sprinkle pepper, along with a bit more salt (Tuscans love salt) on the outside of the roast. Roll it in the rest of the rosemary, garlic mince. Put aside

8. Open the beans. Drain them from their packing water. Rinse them thoroughly. Put aside.

9. Mince two cloves of garlic.

10. Take the Italian plum tomatoes. Cut them into pieces (bite size will do). Put aside.

Final Preparation & Presentation

Carbonara Pasta

When the water for the pasta comes to a rolling boil toss in two tablespoons of salt and half a package of spaghetti (200 grams or 1/2 lb). Make sure to read the cooking time on the package so you drain your pasta *al dente*. While pasta is cooking, pull a large frying pan from the cupboard. Place it on a medium heat burner, toss in the cubed bacon slices and allow them to brown until crispy. Five minutes should do it. I like to toss in a sprig of fresh thyme for the aroma it adds to the kitchen as well as to the dish. When bacon is slightly crispy, but still meaty, turn off the heat.

Once the pasta has reached its *al dente* stage, scoop a cup of starchy water from the pot, drain the pasta and toss the noodles into the bacon. Add the egg and cheese mixture to the pan, along with 1/4 cup of the starchy water. Turn up the heat for a moment (no more than 40 seconds) and mix the noodles into the bacon and egg mixture so all noodles get coated. Add more starchy pasta water if need be to keep noodles moist and creamy. IMPORTANT: the eggs will heat, thus cook, moments after the hot pasta hits them. But if you are concerned about tossing raw yolks into the mix then I suggest using the pasteurized egg yolks that can be found in the dairy section of most supermarkets. But do remember that this delicious *carbonara* pasta is made with farm fresh eggs here in Italy. Serve immediately.

Arista (Pork Loin Roast)

This roast can either be cooked on the stovetop or in the oven. I like stove topping it. But that requires staying in the kitchen to turn it in the pot regularly. So, for those who want to forget about it for 20 minutes or so, before turning it over for another 20 minutes, I suggest going with the oven version below.

Preheat your oven to 375°F. Place the roast on a baking dish lined with foil or parchment paper. Drizzle olive oil over it and pop it in the oven for 20 minutes while you are preparing the beans. Check it after 20 minutes or so and turn it over. I usually pour 1/4 cup of wine over the roast when I turn it. Use the wine you are serving for dinner. If it's good enough for you, it's good enough for your roast! If you are not serving wine, then add a 1/4cup of vegetable or meat broth made from bouillon. A small pork roast takes roughly 35 -40 minutes to cook. Remember Italians cut into pork when it is white and juicy (roughly 155° on a meat thermometer). Before pulling the roast from the oven, I suggest turning on the broiler for a couple of minutes to get a golden crust on the top. Slice the meat into 1/8 inch slices and place on serving tray. Pour juices left in the broiling pan atop. Serve alongside warm bread and the beans here below.

Beans cooked in Tomato & Sage

Take a medium size pot. Pour three tbsp. of olive oil inside. Toss in 2 previously minced garlic cloves. Allow to sauté for a minute or two, until garlic is golden. Add the minced tomatoes and 6 or so fresh sage leaves. Add salt and pepper to taste. Allow tomatoes to simmer for 5 minutes or so in the garlic and oil. Add the previously rinsed beans and 1/4 cup of vegetable broth. Stir. Allow the beans to simmer for 20 minutes or so. Being they are already cooked, they simply need to cook up in the tomato and herb sauce. These beans can also be prepared earlier and re-heated just before serving them alongside the roast. The longer they sit in the garlic, oil, tomato and sage sauce, the better they are!

Forno di rame có li trepiedi

Senior Year - Italian Food Terminology

Planning to adopt 'the Italian way' of eating means understanding or at least familiarizing yourself with some good, wholesome Italian food terminology. That's why I decided to compile a list of words, along with their correct pronunciation. If for no other reason, one can impress that special someone with some savvy Italian!

Al dente (al-DEN-tay) – referred to mainly for pasta. It is when pasta is not too soft, but has a slight resistance to it when you bite into the noodle. Italians always eat their pasta 'al dente' – to the tooth.

Antipasto (ahn-tee-PAHS-toh)- the word literally means 'before the meal.'

Arborio rice (ar-BOR-ree-oh). This is a short, fat grain with high starch content. Grown in Italy, it is the rice used to make creamy risotto.

Arugula (aj-ROO-guh-lah). This peppery mustard flavored green is used in salads and to garnish many summertime dishes. It is a wonderful choice when paired with plum cherry tomatoes, and dressed in Balsamic vinaigrette. It is also known as rugula, rucola and rocket.

Baccalà (bah-kah-LAH) Salted Cod fish. Soaked in water for a few days prior to preparing it. Cod is used in a variety of dishes. In Tuscany it is usually cooked with tomato sauce, garlic, parsley and capers – *Alla Livornese* or Leghorn style.

Birra (BEE-rah) Beer. Mostly drunk when having a pizza. Wine (Vino) is the national all time favorite in this Mediterranean country.

Biscotti (bee-SKOW-tee) Hard almond cookies that have been baked twice (bis). They are first baked in the form of a loaf then sliced and baked separately. Italians dip them in sweet wine (*Vin Santo* – Holy Wine) after a meal. Biscotti are a typical Tuscan dessert originating from Prato, a city near Florence.

Bruschetta (bru-SKEH-tah) Toasted bread with garlic rubbed atop, topped with fresh tomatoes, basil or oregano and drizzled with extra virgin olive oil. This is a great antipasto to serve alongside cold cuts and cured olives.

Calzone (kahl-TSOH-nay) A stuffed pizza.

Canapé (KAN-uh-pay) A slice of bread topped with a condiment (usually a creamy one).

Canola oil (kan-OH-luh) Oil made from rapeseed. It is used a lot for frying here in Italy along with sunflower seed oil.

Carbonara (kar-boh-NAH-rah). Sauce made with eggs, cream, bacon and cheese to be served over a Fettucine noodle.

Cavolo Nero (KAH-voh-loh NEH-roh) Tuscan kale. Grown from fall through winter, this black kale is the prime ingredient in a Tuscan vegetable soup known as *Ribollita*. Tuscans are known for their marvelous thick soups.

Chianti (kee-AHN-tee) – A dry red wine coming from Tuscany, mainly the DOC area between Florence and Siena.

Crostini (kroh-STEE-nee). These are little toasts. Served as antipasti. They are also known as canapés. Tuscan crostini are typically made with minced chicken livers and onions. Yummy!

Del Giorno (dehl ZHOHR-noh) This means 'of the day' and is typically seen on menus. Usually it is a dish the chef decided to make that day which is not normally on the fixed menu.

Dolce (DOHL-chay) or dolci (DOHL-chee). The first means sweet; the latter meaning sweets as in desserts.

Espresso (ehs-PREHS-oh) Strong Italian coffee usually made in small pots where the water shoots up into the finely grained coffee grounds and percolates upwards into the top section of the pot.

Formaggio (for-MAH-zhoh) Cheese.

Forno (FOHR-oh) Oven. *Al forno* means baked in the oven

Fritto (FREE-toh) Fried. *Fritto Misto (MEES-toh)* means a mixed fry and usually refers to bite sizes pieces of meat, fish or vegetables.

Griglia (Gree-lyah) *Alla griglia* means on the grill or barbeque

Mascarpone (mah-skar-POH-nay). This is a double cream from northern Italy. This rich, buttery cream is used to make the world renown TIRAMISU dessert.

Minestra (mih-NES-truh). Soup.

Pasta e Fagioli (PAH-stah eh fah-JYOH-lee) A thick creamy bean soup cooked with a short pasta noodle (or sometimes with broken Tagliatelle egg noodles).

Pâté (Pah-TAY) Although the word is French, it is used in Italian cuisine when speaking of creamy spreads to be served on bread.

Pecorino (peh-kuh-REE-noh) A cheese made from sheep's milk. It can be very soft and creamy with a delicate flavor like Monterey jack OR well seasoned – *stagionato* meaning sharp and pungent.

Porchetta (pohr-KAYT-tah) Slow roasting suckling pig seasoned with fresh rosemary and garlic. It is fairly salty.

Porcino (pohr-CHEE-no) A wild mushroom very popular in Italy. Abundant in late summer and early fall. Porcini can be found in their dried version in many supermarkets worldwide.

Primizie (pree-MEE-zee-AY) First of the season produce. Italians follow the seasons when cooking. So when season's first fruits or vegetables appear in greengrocers they are a big item and many times costly.

Purée (pyuh-RAY) Mashed as in mashed potatoes.

Ribollita (ree-boh-LEE-tah) This hearty Tuscan vegetable soup gets its name because it is twice boiled (ri-bollita). On many winter menus throughout Tuscany, this soup (made with seasonal veggies and day old Tuscan salt-less bread) is a must try!

Risotto (rih-ZAW-toh) Italian rice dish where hot stock is ladled, little by little, into rice seasoned with vegetables, meat or fish. The out-come is a creamy delight.

Salumi (sah-LOU-mee) Italian cold cuts or cured meats: i.e. prosciut-to, salame, soprassata (headcheese), finocchiona etc...

Sauté pan (saw-Tay) A pan with a long handle whose sides are gen-erally higher than those of a frying pan. Used a lot in Italy, especial-ly when making pasta sauces as you can drop the noodles into the pan and mix them in the sauce with ease.

Tacchino (tah-KEE-noh) Turkey. Being Thanksgiving is an America holiday, big turkeys in Italian are not seen much. One is more apt to find turkey breasts and roasting pieces in Italian markets.

Tiramisù (tih-ruh-mee-SOO) This delicious 'pick me up' (literal trans-lation) dessert is made with farm fresh eggs, mascarpone cheese, ladyfinger cookies and espresso coffee. Some toss chocolate shav-ings atop to add to its already heavenly taste.

Tartufo (tahr-TOO-foh) Truffle. This is a fungus or tuber that grows beneath oak and chestnut trees. Hunted by trained dogs and even pigs, it is one of the world's most expensive culinary delights.

Vitello Tonnato (vee-TEHL-loh toh-NAH-toh). Delicious sliced, braised veal topped with a savory tuna spread. Two ingredients that truly marry well despite the fact they might not seem to.

Zabaione (zah-bahl-YOH-nay) A scrumptious combo of egg yolks, Marsala wine and sugar. Used to stuff cream puffs in Tuscany.

So now that you have some words to work and play with. Get ready to start dropping a few during your next Italian meal.

"I hope you enjoy the *formaggio*." "Excuse me while I run to the kitchen to turn off the *forno*." "And for *dolce*, I made a *tiramisu*."

Buon Appetito!

Menu One: Asparagus Soufflé - Roasted Quail Wrapped in Bacon & Herbs - Florentine Peas

Preparation Time: 25 minutes; Cooking Time: 35 minutes

Shopping – Ingredients to pick up

1 bunch of asparagus

2 eggs

Milk (3/4 cup) or ¾ vegetable broth

Parmesan cheese (a tasty cheddar will also do)

Butter

White flour

2 small quails

2 slices of non-smoked bacon

Fresh sage & thyme

Garlic

One small package of frozen green peas

One bunch of Italian parsley

One loaf of French or Italian bread

Advance Preparation

1. Take a dozen asparagus. Clean and cut off the bottom part of the stem until you reach the tender part. Toss the hard, woodsy parts away. Chop the stems into 1inch pieces until you reach the tips. Put stems on one side, tips on the other.

2. Put a pot of water on the burner to boil. When water reaches boiling point, toss in a tbsp. of salt along with the asparagus stems. Allow them to blanch (boil slightly) for 2 to 2 1/2 minutes. Prepare a bowl of cold water (preferably ice water). Pluck the asparagus stems from the hot water with a perforated spoon and toss them into the cold water. This not only stops the cooking, it keeps the veggies vibrant green. Set stems aside. Now do the same with the tips.

3. Take a medium size saucepan. Toss in 2 tablespoons butter. Heat. Now toss in 1 1/2 tablespoons of flour. Mix around until a golden paste is formed. Now take the milk and pour it into the roux (paste). Add a dash of salt and a pinch of nutmeg. Stir as white sauce thickens. If too thick, add a bit more milk or water. If too watery, add another 1/2 table-spoon of flour. Put aside. **Note:** to make a vegetable roux just substitute milk with vegetable broth.

4. Take out a blender. Toss in asparagus stems as well as the white sauce. Add 1/4 cup of Parmesan cheese and a clove

of garlic along with a 1/2 teaspoon of fresh thyme. Give it a whirl. Pour the purée into a mixing bowl.

5. Take 2 eggs. Crack them and allow the yolks to fall into another smaller bowl. Toss the yolks into the purée. Mix well. Set aside.

6. Now whisk the egg whites by hand or with a hand mixer. Allow them to peak. They should be soft. Fold (meaning take a spatula and gently stir) 1/2 of the whites into the purée. Now stir in the remaining egg whites. Set aside.

7. Preheat the oven to 375°F.

8. Take ramekins (these are small baking cups – like cupcake or muffin molds), butter the insides and pour the batter inside. This recipe will fill 4 -6 molds. Put aside until oven is preheated.

9. Clean quails. Salt and pepper on both sides. Stick a couple of fresh sage leaves in each cavity along with 1/2 a garlic clove. Take the bacon strips and wrap each bird in a slab around the middle. Place a sage leaf atop the bacon and tie bird up so that the bacon, sage leaf, wings and legs are all tied close to the breast. Put in a small baking dish, drizzle olive oil atop and put aside.

10. Chop 1 clove of garlic.

11. Take a bunch of fresh parsley, chop off long stems. Mince 2 tablespoons of leafy tops. Set aside.

12. Thaw frozen peas.

13. Take loaf of bread. Cut it down lengthwise. Rub a fresh clove of garlic across both halves. Drizzle the bread abundantly with olive oil and a bit of melted butter. Sprinkle with salt and fresh Thyme leaves. Place on a baking pan and set aside.

Final Preparation & Presentation of

Asparagus Soufflé

The oven should now be preheated. Put the ramekins (or muffin/cupcake molds) on a baking dish. Pop them in the oven and allow them to bake for 20 – 25 minutes. They should rise and be golden on top when it's time to pull them out. Once you pull them from the oven they will most likely collapse in the middle (soufflés do that). No worries. Allow them to cool for a few minutes before serving. Note: These soufflés are to be eaten with a dessert spoon and can be placed on a bed of arugula greens when served.

Quail roasted in Bacon & Herbs

As soon as you pull the soufflés from the oven, pop in the baking dish with the two quails inside. Bake them for about twenty minutes, while enjoying the soufflés and conversation.

Check on them, by opening the oven and pouring 1/4 cup of either vegetable broth or wine onto the birds. Turn them over and allow them to bake for another 10 minutes, until the wine evaporates. Now, move them to the top rack of the oven, turn on the broiler and allow the bacon tied to the breast of the bird to sizzle and get crispy golden. Turn off the oven. Remove the birds. Place them on a serving platter. Cut away the string that was holding them together. Cut each bird in half down the middle, arranging the four halves on the platter. Cut the bacon into at least 3 pieces per slab. Sprinkle the bits, along with pan drippings, atop the birds. Pop the oiled bread under the broiler and allow it to toast for a couple of minutes until it is golden on top. Serve bread alongside quail and peas.

Florentine Peas

Note: these peas can be prepared while the soufflé is in the oven. Just reheat before serving them with the entrée. Take a medium size pan. Add 2 tbsp. olive oil. Toss in garlic and sauté for 2 mins. Toss in peas, chopped parsley, a tsp. salt, a pinch of sugar, a dash of pepper. Add 1/4 cup of warm water. Cover peas and allow them to cook for 20 minutes. Remove the cover, turn up heat and allow peas to cook for another five minutes or until liquid has almost completely evaporated. Serve with entrée and garlic bread.

Menu Two: Steamed Clams Sautéed in Wine & Garlic - Tuna & Artichoke Pasta - Crab Cakes on a Bed of Arugula dressed in a Vinaigrette

Total prep time: 45 minutes; Cooking time 15 minutes

Shopping – Ingredients to pick up

1 lb. fresh clams in their shells

1/2 lb. lump crabmeat

1 bunch of Italian parsley

1 celery stalk

One small white onion

Fresh chives & oregano

1 package of arugula or Italian mix salad greens

Flour (3 tbsp. are needed)

Bread crumbs (1 1/3 cups are needed)

2 eggs

1 bulb of garlic

1 lemon

Olive oil

Red hot pepper flakes

1 small can of tuna (oil or water packed)

1 small jar of marinated artichoke hearts

1 jar of Italian plum tomatoes

1 package of spaghetti (1/2 a pack is enough so check cupboard)

1 loaf of French bread

1 bottle of dry white wine

Advance Preparation

1. Get a large pot with a lid that fits tightly. Drop fresh clams inside. Cover and turn on the heat. DO NOT ADD WATER, just the clams in their shells. Within a couple of minutes the clams will steam open, expelling their own liquid (sea water). Once all the clams have popped open (3-5 minutes should do) turn off heat and leave pot covered. Put aside.

2. Get a chopping board and knife (or electric chopper). Mince parsley together with 2 cloves of fresh garlic. Transfer the mince to a bowl. Put aside.

3. Take loaf of French bread and slice at least 4 one inch slices. Toast slices and put aside for the clam dish.

4. With the same cutting board and knife (or an electric chopper) mince celery stalk, 1/2 a small onion and 1 clove of garlic. Also, chop fresh chives and set aside a tablespoon.

5. Pull out small frying pan. Add 2 tablespoons of oil, toss in 1/2 the garlic and parsley mince and sauté for five minutes or until the onion is limp. Remove from heat and transfer sauté to large mixing bowl. Put the remaining garlic and parsley mince aside for use in making clams.

6. Add lump crabmeat (can crab will do – but drain it from its liquid first) to the sauté.

7. Juice one lemon. Put juice aside and keep the two halves to grate later for zest.

8. Pull out mini primer (hand blender) and a tall glass or container to mix in. Crack one egg into container and rain in a bit of oil. Begin mixing/beating with an up and down movement. Continue to rain in the oil slowly until the mayo becomes creamy. Once it fluffs up add a tbsp. of lemon juice, a dash of salt and a hint of pepper. Taste and add lemon if need be. Put mayo aside or in cover and put in fridge if made ahead of time.

9. Now add breadcrumbs (1 1/4 cups) to bowl of crab and herbs. Crack in one egg, add a tbsp. of chopped chives, then mix all the ingredients together. Add salt and pepper to taste. Now stir in a 1/2cup of the mayo and zest 1/2 of the lemon rind. Add the rest of the breadcrumbs (should be a couple more tablespoons). Mix thoroughly before forming patties. If paddies are not holding together, add more breadcrumbs, if they are too dense, add a bit more mayo. Put the rest of the mayo in a small bowl and refrigerate.

10. Dust paddies lightly with flour and put them on a plate or in the fridge (covered) until time to fry or bake them.

11. Pull out cutting board. Take 3 or 4 artichoke hearts from the jar. Pat them with a napkin to remove the packing oil. Cut each half into halves. Transfer these halves to a small bowl. Sprinkle with one tbsp. of fresh oregano leaves.

12. Mince two cloves of garlic. Put aside for Tuna sauté.

13. Put a large pot of water for pasta on the burner to heat.

Final Preparation & Presentation

Steamed Clams in Wine & Garlic

Take a large frying pan (or better yet a sauté pan – one with a higher rim). Add 1/4 cup of olive oil and remaining garlic parsley mince prepared earlier and sauté for a minute or so. Open a can of Italian plum tomatoes. Drain the tomato water (juice) into the sauté with one of the Italian plum tomatoes. Keep the remaining tomatoes aside for the next dish (Tuna Pasta). Allow the tomato juice to simmer for 2 or 3 minutes. Turn off heat.

Uncover clams. One by one, check to see if they are harboring any sand in their shells. If so, rinse the sand out before tossing each sand free clam in its shell into the sauté pan. Once all clams are in the pan, strain the clam juice into the pan by placing a paper towel in a tea strainer and allowing the juice to rain into the sauté. This will keep any sandy residue from spoiling your sauté. No one likes to grind teeth with sand! Turn heat back on the clams and sauté. Once a boiling point is reached season with red hot pepper flakes (if you like spicy), taste for salt (remember clam juice is already salty) and add a dash of pepper. Stir and turn off heat. The result is a pot of freshly steamed clams resting in roughly a cup of liquid. If the liquid seems to have evaporated too much, add a bit more clam juice. Note: you can prepare clams an hour ahead of serving time.

Just make sure to have a bit more clam juice aside so when you quickly reheat the sauté you can add a bit more juice. Sprinkle chopped parsley atop. Serve these savory sautéed clams in individu-al bowls atop the previously toasted bread slices. Make sure to rub a bit of fresh garlic atop each slice and lightly drizzle them with olive oil before dishing the clams and its juice on top.

NOTE: make sure you have an empty bowl sitting on the table so that you and your date can toss the empty shells into it. Remember you will be eating these savory clams with your fingers.

FACT: A rich source of iron, and low in calories, clams contain more protein than red meat, making them a great choice in building lean body mass.

Tuna & Artichoke Pasta

In another large frying pan, add 1/4 cup of olive oil and the two cloves of minced garlic prepared earlier and sauté for a minute. Toss in the canned tomatoes, sprinkle with salt and pepper and hot red pepper flakes. Allow sauce to simmer for 12-15 minutes. Now, open a can of tuna and drain packing liquid (water or oil). Toss tuna into sauce and allow it to simmer for 10 minutes before tossing in artichoke hearts and a tsp. of fresh oregano. Allow the lot to con-tinue simmering for another 5 minutes. Note: this sauce can also be made ahead of time and reheated when pasta is cooked.

By this time your water should have reached a rolling boil. Toss in 2 tablespoons of salt and the pasta noodles. Allow them to cook to an almost *al dente* stage since you will be tossing them into the sauce and allowing them to cook a minute longer. Remember to keep a cup of the starchy pasta water aside before draining noodles. You might need to add a tad of the hot starchy pasta water to your sauce when mixing the noodles in. Starchy pasta water does miracles in creamy up a dish. If minced parsley is still around, toss a bit atop for garnish. Serve.

Crab Cakes

Either put a frying pot on the stove or preheat the oven to 375°F. If baking rather than frying, put cakes onto a baking sheet and pop them into the oven for 20 – 25 minutes. Pull them out when they are golden. If frying, fry until crispy and golden and drain on paper towel. Prepare individual serving plates with a bed of Italian greens. Place cakes atop (two medium cakes per person or 3 smaller cakes). Remove the mayo from the fridge and top each cake with a spoonful. Take one of the lemon rinds you have sitting around and grate zest atop each cake. Serve with warm Tuscan or French bread.

NOTE: I would have a light oil and vinaigrette on the table to dress salad beneath the crab cakes. When serving, you could also position the salad to the side of the cakes as opposed to having the cakes sit on the bed of greens that way dress the salad and it enjoy it with the crab cakes.

Menu Three: Mushroom & Sausage Pasta - Pork Wellington - Oven Baked Herb Potatoes

Preparation time: 15 min; Cooking & baking time 45-55 min

Shopping – Ingredients to pick up

One pork loin roast (1lb is plenty but most likely you'll find at least 2 lb. trunks, so divide the roast into two pieces and freeze one OR cook the entire roast and slice it for sandwiches during the week.

Two Italian sausages

1 package of dried porcini mushrooms (if unavailable, cultivated mushrooms will do – pick up about 10)

One yellow onion (medium size)

Fresh rosemary, thyme, sage & bay leaves (2)

2 large white or red potatoes

Olive oil

1 bulb of garlic

Vegetable broth (granular, bouillon or stock)

1 - 14.28 oz. can of Italian plum tomatoes (without added herbs)

1 loaf of French or Italian Bread

1 package of penne pasta (1/2 a pack is enough so check cupboard)

Parmesan cheese (grated) optional

Parchment paper or aluminum foil

Advance Preparation

1. Take your piece of roast. Poke half a dozen holes in it with a sharp knife. Put aside for a moment.

2. Take out a cutting board and knife, or the electric chopper. Mince garlic and 2 tbsp. of fresh rosemary leaves. Now sprinkle salt (1 tbsp.) onto the mince, add a dash of pepper, mix and stuff the holes in the roast. Roll the meat in the mince that is left. Set aside for a moment.

3. Take your loaf of French or Italian bread. Now check to see how long your roast is and cut the bread the same length (or a bit longer) as the roast. Take bread and cut it down the middle lengthwise. Now gut out each half of the bread's doughy center using your hand. This will create a crater in each half. Drizzle olive oil in each crater, take the seasoned pork loin and place it in one of the craters. Cover the meat with the other half loaf. It will create a sandwich. Pull out kitchen string or sturdy thread. Wrap it around the bread, so the meat is snug inside the two halves. Tie it up and set it aside.

4. Put dried Italian porcini mushrooms in a bowl of warm water and allow them to soak for at least 30 minutes. They will quickly soften and swell. If you opted for fresh mushrooms. Clean the mushrooms and slice them into pieces.

5. Chop one small yellow onion (half if it is big), and two cloves of garlic. Set aside.

6. Peel potatoes (2 good size ones should be enough). Cut them into bite size pieces. Place them in a bowl of water and set aside.

7. Put a large pot of water on the stovetop to heat

8. Preheat the oven to 375°F.

Final Preparation & Presentation

Oven Baked Herb Potatoes
Remove potatoes from water. Pat them dry. Now take a baking sheet, line it with parchment paper or aluminum foil (parchment is better). Toss the potatoes on the paper, drizzle them with olive oil. Toss four or five sage leaves, some fresh rosemary thickets and a bay leaf or two. Using hands, mix potatoes in the oil and herbs until all potatoes are coated. Now pop them into a 350°F preheated oven. If you are popping them in the same time as the roast, make

sure you alternate shelves (roast on top for 20 minutes, potatoes on bottom) then visa versa. Pull potatoes out after 20 minutes and move them around a bit on the paper, sprinkling salt and pepper on top. If they are too soft and begin to break, pop them back inside the oven and allow them to get golden on the top before turning them over. They will take roughly 40 -45 minutes to bake in a traditional oven. A bit less if the oven is ventilated. They are done when golden all around. Taste for salt. Serve alongside pork Wellington.

Pork Wellington

Once the oven reaches a temperature of 375°F (180°c) put your roast encased in bread on a baking sheet lined with parchment paper or in a baking dish. Slip it into the oven (covered with foil), for 20 minutes. Pull it out of the oven and pour 1/4 cup of white wine or vegetable broth over the bread crust, this will keep it moist and not allow the crust to burn or get too crispy too early. Put back in oven another 15 minutes or until crust gets golden and meat is juicy. Check to see if it needs basting to keep bread a bit moist. Pull it out again and turn it over. Allow another 5 minutes of baking before turning the oven off. It will finish cooking in warm oven. Remember pork loin takes roughly 20-25 minutes per pound to reach an internal temperature of 155 to 160°F. If you have a meat thermometer stick it into the middle of the roast 30 minutes into baking to check temp. Allow the roast to sit for 10 min before cutting. This allows juices to run into inner part of bread. Remove the string and slice bread and pork into 11/2inch slices. Serve alongside potatoes.

Mushroom & Sausage Pasta

Take a medium size sauté pan. Add 1/4 cup of olive oil, the minced onion, 1 clove of minced garlic, 1 teaspoon of fresh thyme and sauté the lot on a medium to low heat until the onion is limp and transparent. Now take the two sausages. Squeeze the rosy pork out of its casing and toss it into the sauté. Allow the pork to cook in the onion and herbs for 3 or 4 minutes, until it turns beige. Now toss in the mushrooms. If you are using the dried porcini, toss in the previously soaked mushrooms and put the water aside. If, on the other hand, you are using fresh mushrooms toss them into the sauté and allow them to cook with the sausage for about 5 minutes. Now toss in the Italian plum tomatoes along with a few bay leaves. Cover the pot and allow the sauce to simmer for 20 minutes. Uncover, taste for salt and pepper. IF sauce is dense, add a couple of tablespoons of the mushroom water. Stir and continue to simmer for 6 minutes.

The pasta water has surely come to a rolling boil by now. Toss in 2 tablespoons of salt along with the pasta. Allow pasta to cook (look at cooking time on the package) to the *al dente* stage. Drain pasta, keeping a 1/2cup of the starchy pasta water aside as it may be needed. Now toss the drained noodles into the sauce and mix, allowing the sauce to coat each and every noodle. If need be, add a bit of the starchy pasta water. Serve with or without grated cheese.

Note: As you are cooking the pasta, your roast and potatoes should have already gone into the oven some thirty minutes prior. That way they will be just about ready when you have finished enjoying the pasta. Alternative. Keep roast and potatoes in a warm oven if prepared before the pasta.

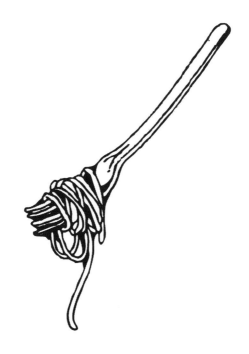

Menu Four: Asparagus Risotto (with shrimp) - Grilled Beef Sautéed in Rosemary & Green Peppercorns - Sautéed Spinach

Preparation time: 30 min; Cooking time: 20 – 25 min

Shopping – Ingredients to pick up

One bunch of asparagus

1 cup of shrimp

1 cup of Arborio rice or any small, fat grain rice with a high starch content (ex: Vialone Nano or Carnaroli)

2 pints of vegetable broth (granular, stock or bouillon)

Note: bouillon – 4 cubes; granular 4 teaspoons.

Olive oil

Butter (2 tablespoons)

One medium white onion

One bulb of garlic

2 tender steak fillets

Fresh rosemary & thyme

Green Peppercorns (in brine is better than dry)

Salt & Pepper

1 package of frozen spinach

1 loaf of French or Italian bread

Parmesan cheese (optional for risotto)

Advance Preparation

1. Rinse asparagus and cut off the woodsy bottom stems. Toss them away before cutting off the tips and chopping the tender stem into bite size pieces. Toss stems into a pot of boiling water (lightly salted) and allow them to boil for 3 minutes. Remove them from the boiling water and toss them into a bowl of ice water. This stops the cooking and keeps them green. Do the same to the tips. Then put them aside. They will be used at the end. If adding shrimp to the asparagus, clean the crustaceans and put them aside.

2. Pull out a cutting board or electric chopper. Toss in one clove of garlic and the onion. Mince fine. Put aside.

3. Take a bowl. Fill it with 1/4 cup of olive oil. Toss in a table-spoon of green peppercorns. Add 2 tablespoons of fresh rosemary thickets. Add a dash of salt and a crack of pepper.

Allow the ingredients to marry (marinate) for at least 30 minutes.

4. Mince 3 more cloves of garlic (two for the spinach and one for the bread).

5. Thaw spinach

6. Put a quart of vegetable broth on the stovetop to heat. Note: one bouillon cube makes 8 oz (there are 32 oz to a quart), thus toss 3 to 4 cubes in a quart of water and let boil. If you are using granular stock toss in 4 teaspoons of stock to one quart of water.

7. Pull out grill for steaks. Or get barbeque ready.

Final Preparation & Presentation

Risotto (Porcini Mushroom OR Asparagus)
Pull out a medium pot. Toss in 2 tablespoons of oil and two table-spoons of butter. Heat. Now toss in minced onion and garlic clove. Once onion becomes transparent and limp (4 minutes or so) toss in asparagus pieces (not tips). You will toss them at the end along with the shrimp if you opted to add the tasty sea creatures.

Allow the vegetables to sauté for two minutes. Now ladle in 1/4 cup of broth, turn heat to a medium low and allow the vegetables to simmer for 20 minutes or so. If need be, ladle in a bit more broth.

Toss in the rice and stir. Keep stirring for a minute or two or until the kernels begin sticking to the bottom of the pot. Now ladle in broth (roughly 1/2 cup). Stir. Rice will grow to twice its volume so be prepared to ladle in more broth every few minutes for 16 to 18 minutes (depending on the cooking time on package). Remember rice should be *al dente*.

Important: About 10 minutes into the cooking, toss in the asparagus tips. Then 13 minutes or so into the cooking, toss in a cup of fresh shrimp.

After the last ladle of broth (16 minutes or so into cooking) cover the rice and turn off the heat.* It will continue to steam cook for another couple of minutes. Serve in individual dishes.

*NOTE: Some cooks add a tablespoon of butter or heavy cream at this point if the rice doesn't seem creamy enough. This is usually due to a lesser starch content in the rice.

Grilled Beef Sautéed in Rosemary & Peppercorns

Heat the grill or barbeque. Toss the fillets on the fire or heat and allow them to grill on both sides. Sprinkle with salt and pepper as you turn the meat over.

While the fillets are grilling, add olive oil, rosemary and green peppercorns to a small pot and heat up the oil and herbs for a minute, no longer. Take out a cutting board and knife. Take the grilled fillets and slice them into strips. Place the strips on a serving platter and pour the warm oil, rosemary and peppercorns atop. Serve along-side sautéed spinach.

Sautéed Spinach

Take a medium sized frying pan. Add two tablespoons of olive oil. Toss in two minced garlic cloves. Allow garlic to sauté for a minute or two in the rich oil. Toss in the thawed spinach (squeeze out all excess liquid before tossing into the pan). Salt and pepper the spin-ach. Stir and cover. Allow spinach to simmer for 10 minutes. If greens seem too dry, add a tbsp. of vegetable broth or warm water and allow it to evaporate. Serve sautéed spinach alongside the steak and a basket of warm bread. You can also add a nice salad. Remember, Italian have salad at the end of their meals not at the beginning.

Let's Talk Dessert

Italian desserts, like its cuisine in general, follow the seasons as much as traditions. For example, at Christmastime you will find two desserts taking center stage on Italian tables: *panforte* (pan-FOHR-the) - a tasty almond fruitcake; and *panettone* (pan-uh-TOH-nee). The latter being a sweet, yeast bread filled with raisin and candied citrus. But once the doors of the Yuletide season close on the evening January 6th (the Epiphany), these two desserts disappear until the next Christmas season.

But what comes in to take their place? Well, the forty days leading up to Easter means Carnival time in Italy. And with all this merry-making, two desserts parade in. This is the time of year that almost every Florentine pastry shop window showcases *schiacciata alla Fiorentina*, a type of citrus yeast *focaccia* (foh-KAH-chyah) with a hint of orange zest, smothered in powdered sugar. The other delight you will find this time of year is *cenci* (lightly fried strips of sweet dough dusted with powdered sugar).

But as soon as Easter Sunday knocks on the door, these two desserts like *panforte* and *panettone* at Christmas, make their retreat, for it is time for *La Colomba*. But like the others, this dove shaped, orange flavored sweet bread covered in toasted almonds isn't the only treat riding on the breezes of spring.

For as soon as strawberries and cherries find their way to vegetable and fruit markets, an array of tangy fruit tarts make their way into pastry shop windows. From May to November these tasty fruit desserts, many paired with rich cream, share center stage with creamy Italian gelatos.

As summer comes to an end, and the first signs of autumn show its face, *castagnaccio* (a tasty flat cake made with chestnut flour, pine nuts and raisins), rolls in with the season's low lying fog. This is an unusual semi-sweet dessert that carries the aroma of autumn in every bite.

Apart from these seasonal delights, there are a few staple desserts that can be found all year round. Probably the most common, at least in Tuscany, is *biscottini* di Prato (bee-SKO-tee-knee). These hard almond cookies are paired with sweet wine (Vin Santo). But just as popular is the infamous *tiramisù* (tih-rah-mee-SOO). A creamy dessert made with ladyfinger cookies soaked in coffee and smothered in a rich mascarpone cream.

But let us not forget an all time favorite: *profiterole* (proh-FIH-ter-ohl), or better known as BONGO BONGO. These golf ball size puff pastries stuffed with fresh cream and smothered in a rich dark chocolate sauce are delicious. As is another sublime chocolate delight that has taken the spotlight lately – chocolate flourless tarts (see recipe). Top them with cream and they are heavenly!

The Chosen Three: Chocolate Flourless Tarts - Seasonal Fruit Smothered in Pastry Cream - Tiramisù

Chocolate Flourless Tarts or Cake
Prep Time: 10 min; Baking time: 14 -16 min

The recipe below makes roughly 12 small tarts

Shopping – Ingredients to pick up
1 1/4 cups unsweetened dark chocolate

1/2 cup of butter

1 cup of powdered sugar

3 eggs

Work Plan & Preparation
Take two saucepans (one that will comfortably sit inside the other). Reason being: you will be filling the larger one 1/4 full with water before sitting the smaller one inside (double boiler). Just make sure when you put the smaller one inside that the water in the larger one doesn't flow over onto the stove. Now put the chocolate squares and butter into the smaller pot on top and cover pot. Turn on the heat. Once the water surrounding the smaller pot begins to boil the

chocolate and butter will melt in the top pot, forming a dense chocolate cream. Stir until chocolate and butter are completely melted and uniform. Set aside for a moment.

Take an electric beater and a large bowl. Crack the eggs in the bowl. Add the powdered sugar and beat together until the eggs have incorporated all the sugar. Now slowly incorporate the chocolate and butter cream into the egg mixture, stirring with a large wooden spoon. Mix the batter on a low speed for a minute or until you have a homogenous batter. Grease the cupcake molds with butter or oil then flour dust them (this means pouring a bit of flour into the greased mold and tipping it here and there until all the oil is dusted. Now pour in the batter.

Preheat oven to 325°F (160°C) and bake cupcakes for 14 – 16 min. or until they rise and begin to slightly crack on top. Remove the tarts from the oven and allow them to cool. Remember, being they are soufflés they will tend to drop in the middle.

No worries... just fill these craters with a fresh strawberry or julienne orange peels. Then sprinkle powdered sugar atop. To make them richer yet, serve alongside a scoop of freshly whipped cream.

***

Fresh Fruit Smothered in Pastry Cream

Prep time: 15 mins; Cooking time: 20 min

Shopping – Ingredients to pick up

1 basket of fresh berries (mixed or one kind) OR 3 - 4 fresh peaches

Milk (1 1/4 cups are needed)

Vanilla (powdered or liquid – only 1/2 teaspoon is needed)

3 eggs

White sugar (1/4 cup is needed)

Flour (1/8 cup is needed)

Cornstarch (3 tablespoons is needed)

Work Plan & Preparation

In a medium-sized stainless steel bowl, mix sugar and egg yolks to-gether with a wooden spoon before adding flour and cornstarch. Mix until a smooth paste forms. Set aside. In a saucepan, heat milk and vanilla on medium heat until boiling point is reached. Remove from heat and slowly rain in flour. Add egg mixture and whisk to prevent cream from curdling. Return mixture to heat and allow it to reach boiling point once more. Keep whisking.

Gradually, the mixture will became harder and harder to stir. Remove custard from heat and transfer to a large bowl. Cover with plastic wrap and allow it to cool. Note: custard can be kept in refrigerator for a couple of days.

Clean fresh berries or peaches. Cut into bite size pieces and place in individual bowls. Smother the fruit with the pastry cream. Serve.

Tiramisù

Prep time: 25 minutes – Allow dessert to sit at least 30 – 45 minutes in fridge before serving.

Some might shy away from making *tiramisù* because the idea of using raw, farm fresh uncooked eggs might present worry. No worries, those who prefer to not use farm fresh eggs can substitute the fresh with already pasteurized eggs found in cartons in the dairy section of most supermarkets. Just buy the pasteurized yolks and substitute the whites with 8 oz. of heavy cream.

Shopping- Ingredients to pick up
4 eggs

Granulated sugar (3/4 cup is needed)

Vanilla (1 teaspoon is needed)

8 oz (one cup) of mascarpone

8 oz (one cup) heavy cream (if substituting whites for cream)

1 package of ladyfinger cookies

Chocolate chips (1/2 a cup is need)

Coffee (preferably Italian) – 2 cups brewed – slightly sugared

Cacao (optional) or chocolate shavings for garnish

Work Plan & Preparation
Make a pot of Italian coffee (2 cups). Sugar the coffee as you please. Set aside.

Separate eggs (yolks from whites). Beat the yolks with 1/2 of the sugar until creamy. Add the mascarpone to the mix stirring with a wooden spoon until it is incorporated enough to start mixing with electric mixture. Beat until you have a dense yellow cream. Set aside. In another bowl, beat the eggs whites until they peak, adding the remaining sugar little by little.

If you opted to use the pasteurized yolks, and substitute the whites with the cream, then whip the cream. Now pour the peaked egg whites and sugar (or cream and sugar) mixture into the mascarpone and egg yolk cream. Fold in the whites (meaning do not use the mixture but a spatula) mix slowly until a homogenous velvety cream is obtained. Put aside.

Take out a baking dish (preferably rectangular).

Get ladyfinger cookies. Dip the cookies into the coffee one by one before lining the baking dish with these coffee bathed cookies. Once the bottom of the baking dish is lined with the first rows of cookies, pour the scrumptious cream atop. Repeat the operation with a second layer of coffee drenched cookies then another blanket of velvety cream. Sprinkle chocolate chips atop the last layer of cream. Lightly sift cacao atop. Cover with a plastic wrap and refrigerate until ready to serve.

Note: This is a great dessert to make either in the morning or afternoon and let chill before serving in the evening.

\

A Tasty Dessert Option

Cheese & Fruit

Italians almost always finish their meals with either a dessert or fresh fruit (sometimes even both). If you plan on serving both, serve the dessert first and the fruit after. Many times, when fruit is served as dessert, a cheese tray with honey or interesting marmalades accompany it. Italians, unlike North Americans, generally serve cheese at the end of the meal as opposed to offering it as an antipasto. However, with globalization, you may find a few trendy Italian restaurants up and down the boot adopting the North American custom of serving cheese alongside a platter of *salumi* (cold cuts) as an antipasto.

But, if you want to add that 'European' flair to the end of your meal, and don't have time to make dessert, then offer your guest(s) a creamy or aged sheep cheese to be enjoyed with a dabble of sticky, sweet honey. It's the perfect way to end a meal.

A Word about Wine Pairing

Wine is relished, as much as the food it is served with. Italians are very traditional when it comes to pairing their drinks with their food. They tend to pair white wine with white food, red wine with meats and beer with pizza... Meaning you will usually find dry or fruity white wines served with fish or poultry. In summer a chilled white wine is usually paired with the seasonal array of veggies. Whereas a red wine, whether bold or mellow, is commonly paired with meat; beef and pork. A good rule of thumb is: the redder the meat, the bolder the wine.

But how about when it comes to vegetarian meals? I believe it's all in one's preference. A stuffed eggplant swimming in a spicy red sauce marries well with a mellow red, as does a porcini mushroom risotto, at least in my kitchen. Though some prefer a dry white with mushrooms. An artichoke *frittata,* on the other hand, pairs well with a crisp acidic white. Although some wine experts believe artichokes and wine in general don't bring out the best in one another. Reason: artichokes tend to sweeten the taste of wine. However, it is my belief that if you prepare your palate with, let's say a tangy *Pinot Grigio*, before treating your taste buds to the wonderful flavor of artichokes, the result will surely be harmonizing.

When it comes to starting the evening, it isn't uncommon to serve a bubbly white wine (*Prosecco*) with antipasti, especially when you are serving finger foods while mingling and conversing. But this nose tickling delight may also be paired with dessert.

Conclusion: no matter which wine, if any, you choose to pair with these menus, just remember that moderation is the key. Italians tend to calculate 1/4 of a bottle of wine per person at any given meal. That's savoring the wine, savoring the meal, savoring the moment. Remember there's always a bottle of water (sparkling or still) on Italian tables as well, for those who prefer pairing their meal with water: a smooth liquid that elevates the aroma and taste of dishes without masking flavors. Saltier waters go great with chocolate desserts. Still water pairs with meats while slightly effervescent water is perfect for salads or poultry.
A sparkling water (like Prosecco), is the perfect companion for antipasti.

Whether you pair wine or water with these dishes, my hope is that you will savor every bite. Enjoy!

About the Author

I moved to Italy in 1979 from my native California. The first twelve years of my Italian life were spent in a renovated 18th century farmhouse in Tuscany's Chianti wine region. It was there, thanks to the moms and grandmothers of the countryside, that I developed an insatiable passion for the region's simple, yet exquisitely fresh cuisine.

In 1992, after purchasing and renovating a property within the walls of a medieval citadel, my husband and I left the countryside for life in the ancient hamlet. The next four years we spent soaking up Tuscan village life while raising our two sons. When the boys came of school age we made one last move, this time to my husband's native Florence, where we reside.

My husband and I share an avid passion for good food and wines. Our passion has taken us on countless food jaunts around the globe. "Food memories are the spice of life," we say. Being a culinary instructor, I am always happy to organize private dining experiences for foodies who share our philosophy: good food and wine, coupled with stimulating conversations is what makes life worth living. So if you find yourself in Florence... look us up. (sindyfirenze@yahoo.com)

MENU TWO: TUNA CANAPÉS - HOMEMADE PESTO PASTA - BROILED FISH (TILAPIA OR OTHER FISH FILLET) SMOTHERED IN GRILLED VEGGIES   35

AMATRICIANA (BACON & ONION) SPAGHETTI-GRILLED PORK MEDALLIONS ON PEPPERY ARUGULA   40

MENU TWO: *BRUSCHETTA* - PESTO PASTA BAKE – RICOTTA STUFFED EGGPLANT IN TOMATO SAUCE82

MENU THREE: STUFFED MUSHROOMS - GRILLED MEAT/VEGETABLE KABOBS & HERB BAKED POTATOES   88

Made in the USA
Middletown, DE
12 May 2019